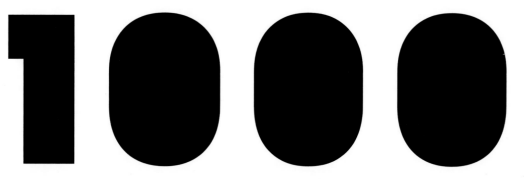

1000

icons, symbols + pictograms
1,000 works selected by BLACKCOFFEE

ROCKPORT

1,000 works selected by BLACKCOFFEE

ROCKPORT PUBLISHERS

1000

icons, symbols + pictograms
Visual Communications for Every Language

© 2006 by Rockport Publishers, Inc.

First published in the United States of America by
Rockport Publishers, Inc., a member of
Quayside Publishing Group
33 Commercial Street
Gloucester, Massachusetts 01930-5089
Telephone: (978) 282-9590
Fax: (978) 283-2742
www.rockpub.com

ISBN 10: 1-59253-239-X
ISBN 13: 978-1-59253-239-1

10 9 8 7 6 5 4 3 2 1

Design: Blackcoffee® (Boston, MA)

Printed in China

To all the companies around the globe who shared their work, thank you.

Thanks to the folks at Rockport Publishers for their help, support, and collaboration throughout this process.

We'd also like to thank Tim Gillman for photography, Andrea Fugere, and Jocelin Johnson.

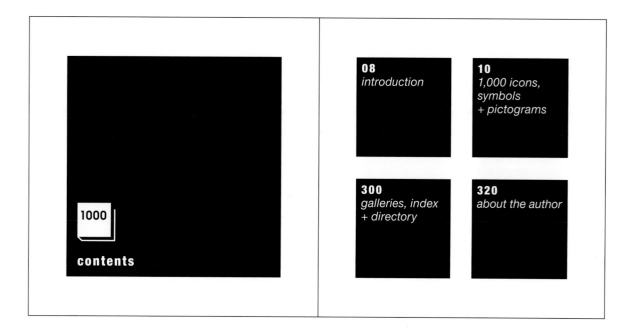

1000

contents

INTRODUCTION

WHY THIS IS IMPORTANT

Picture yourself in an airport, in a foreign country. You've just landed. You don't speak the language. You don't know the culture. You are, in effect, lost. Despite the language you speak or where you're from, first aid is first aid, food is food, luggage is luggage, and transportation is transportation. Without this symbolic language, you would be confused and bewildered and may never find your way.

Icons, symbols, and pictograms may be the purest form of visual communication. They transcend the boundaries of language and culture to convey a concept quickly and effectively. In selecting the works to be featured in this book, we sought out simple, elegant solutions that communicated information clearly—something we call simplexity. As we filtered through the piles of submissions and collected works, we learned a great deal about icon design and cross-cultural communication. We hope that you also leave this book with a new appreciation for the world of icons, symbols, and pictograms.

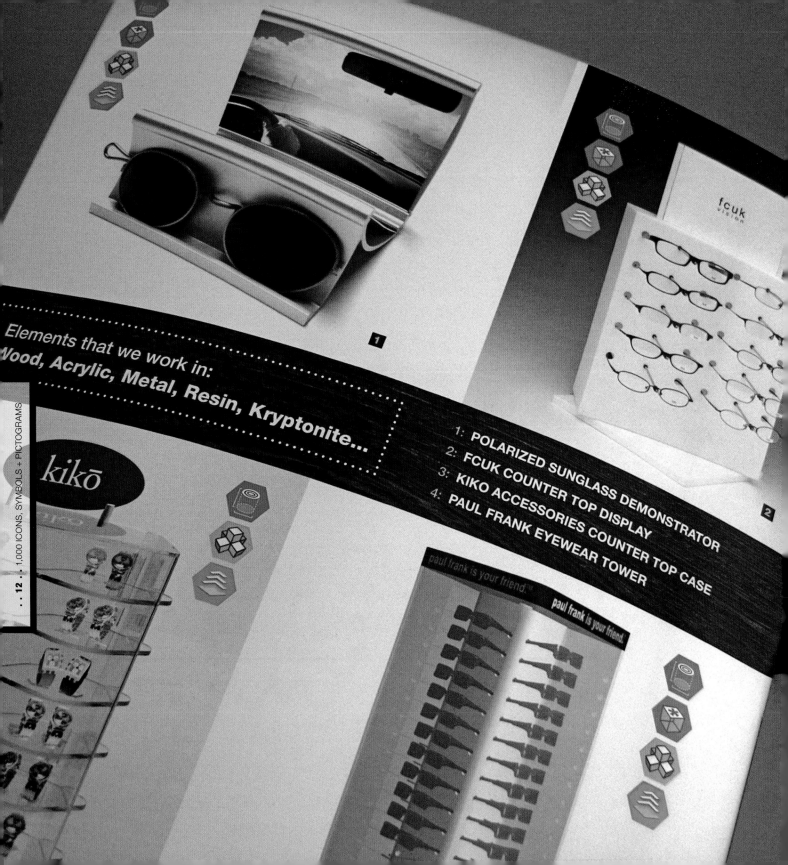

Elements that we work in:
Wood, Acrylic, Metal, Resin, Kryptonite...

kikō

1: POLARIZED SUNGLASS DEMONSTRATOR
2: FCUK COUNTER TOP DISPLAY
3: KIKO ACCESSORIES COUNTER TOP CASE
4: PAUL FRANK EYEWEAR TOWER

fcuk
vision

paul frank is your friend.™
paul frank is your friend.™

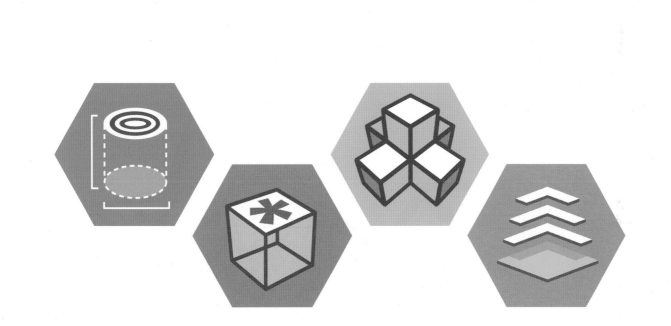

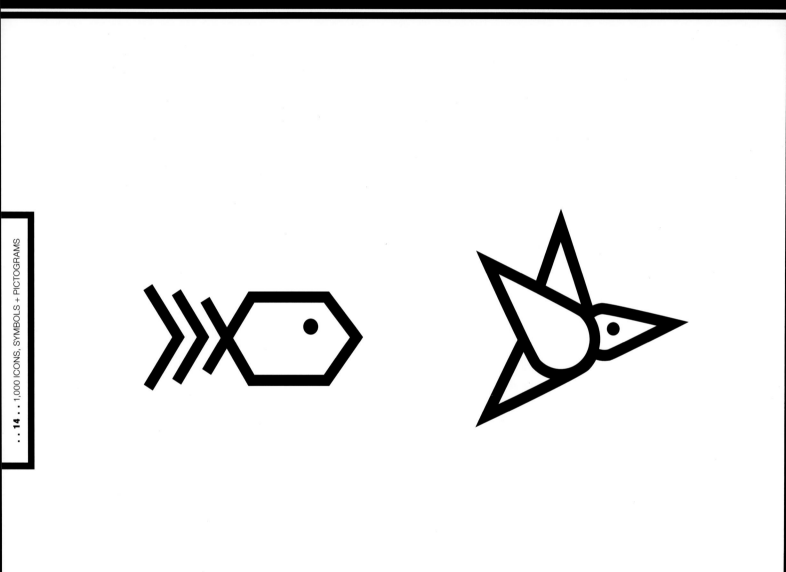

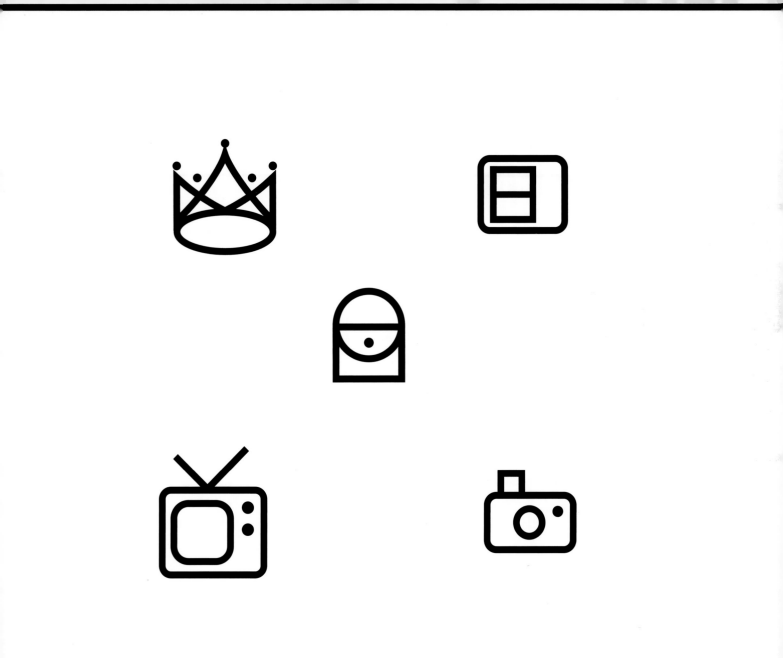

0020–0026
Gardner Design ~ USA
client ~ Gardner Design

...logical wherewithal not only to understand what
...environmental distress, but also to find practical solutions.
...knowledge and resources at our disposal to create a safer, more
...sustainable life for all the world's citizens."

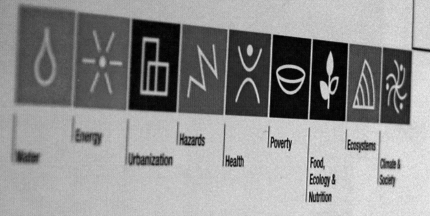

Water Energy Urbanization Hazards Health Poverty Food, Ecology & Nutrition Ecosystems Climate & Society

The Cross-Cutting Themes

Earth Institute scholars work in teams across disciplines
in the natural, social and physical sciences to conduct
research and forge interdisciplinary solutions to complex
global problems.
The themes: water, energy, urbanization, hazards, health,
poverty, ecosystems, climate, and food-ecology-nutrition.
The goal: to transfer and scale up the lessons of one
project on similar efforts around the globe.

...Columbia University is among the
...centers for the integrated study of
...and society. The Earth Institute builds
...core disciplines—earth sciences,
...engineering sciences, social sciences
...cross-disciplinary
...Through research, train-
...nurtures science and tech-
...while placing

The Earth Clinic

The Earth Institute @ Columbia University ~ USA
client ~ The Earth Institute @ Columbia University

0027–0035
The Earth Institute @ Columbia University ~ USA
client ~ The Earth Institute @ Columbia University

. . **20** . . 1,000 ICONS, SYMBOLS + PICTOGRAMS

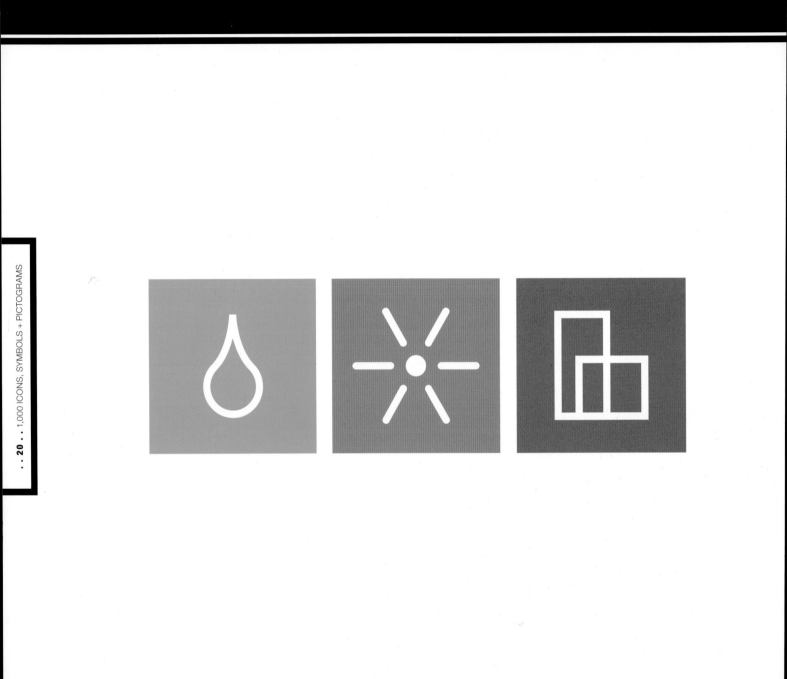

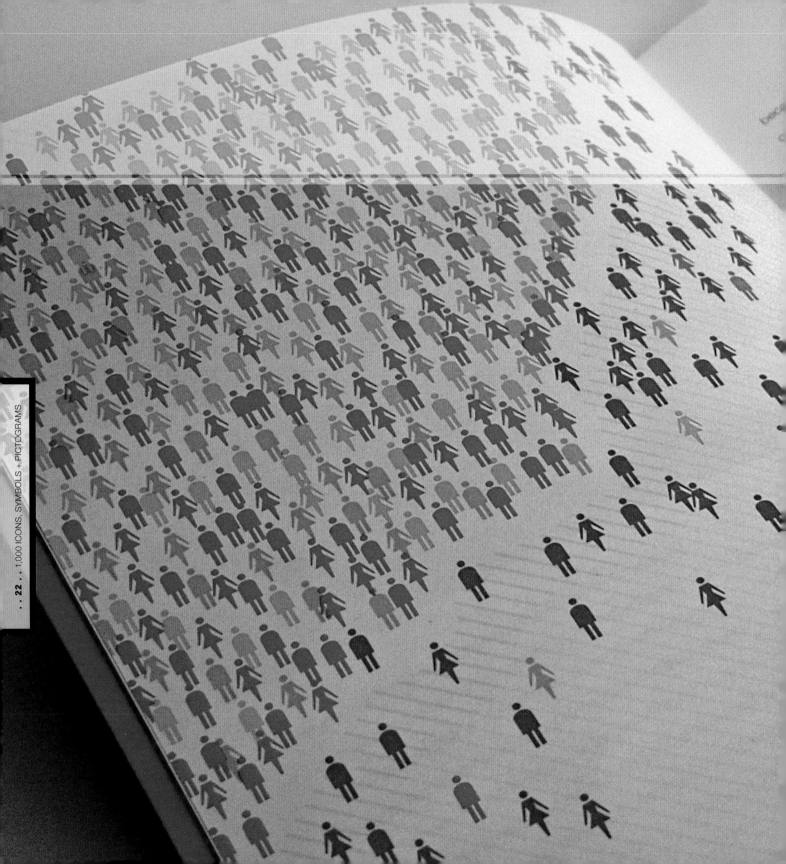

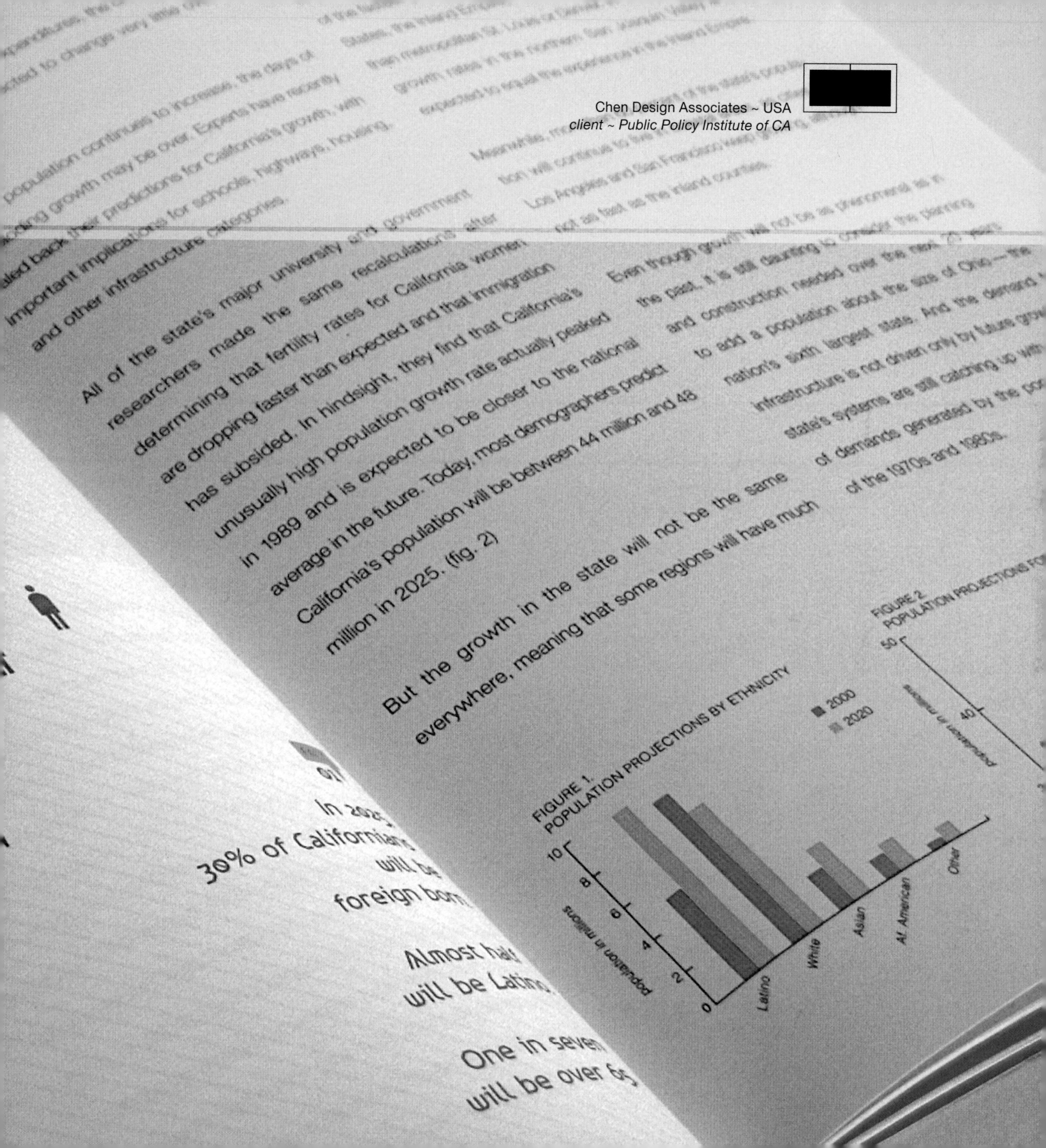

Chen Design Associates ~ USA
client ~ Public Policy Institute of CA

All of the state's major university and government researchers made the same recalculations after determining that fertility rates for California women are dropping faster than expected and that immigration has subsided. In hindsight, they find that California's unusually high population growth rate actually peaked in 1989 and is expected to be closer to the national average in the future. Today, most demographers predict California's population will be between 44 million and 48 million in 2025. (fig. 2)

Even though growth will not be as phenomenal as in the past, it is still daunting to consider the planning and construction needed over the next 25 years to add a population about the size of Ohio—the nation's sixth largest state. And the demand for infrastructure is not driven only by future growth; state's systems are still catching up with the set of demands generated by the population of the 1970s and 1980s.

But the growth in the state will not be the same everywhere, meaning that some regions will have much

In 2025, 30% of Californians will be foreign born

Almost half will be Latino

One in seven will be over 65

FIGURE 1.
POPULATION PROJECTIONS BY ETHNICITY

FIGURE 2.
POPULATION PROJECTIONS FOR

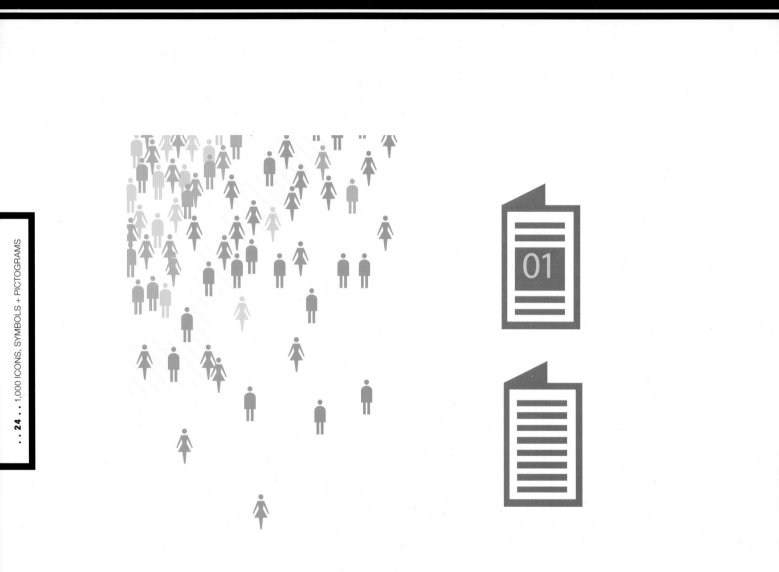

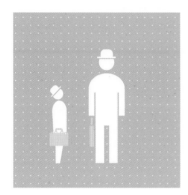

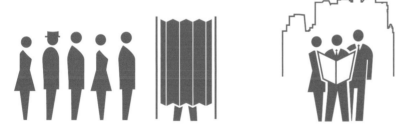

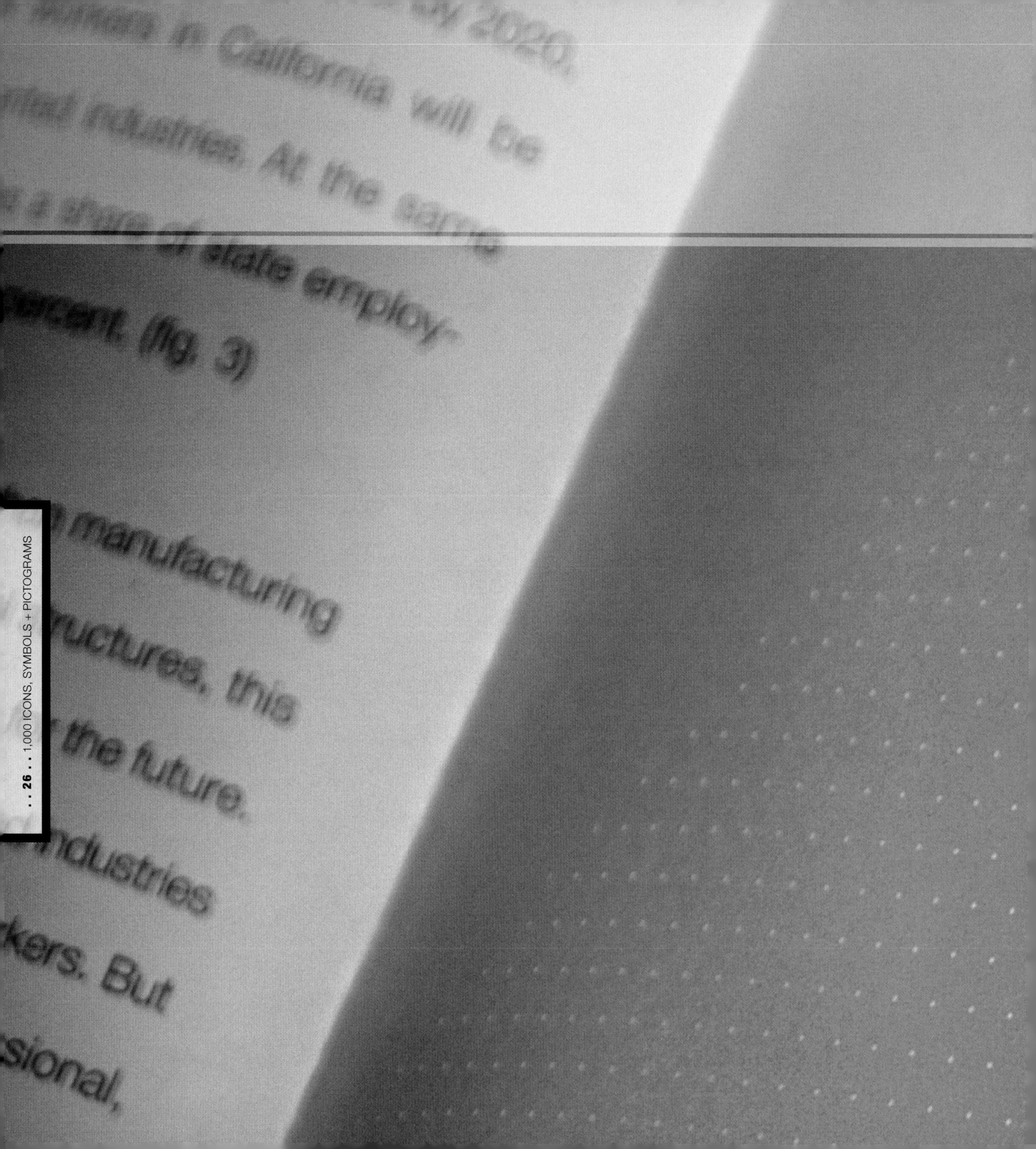

2020,

workers in California will be

ified industries. At the same

a share of state employ-

ercent. (fig. 3)

manufacturing

ructures, this

the future.

industries

rkers. But

sional,

Chen Design Associates ~ USA
client ~ Public Policy Institute of CA

0045—0050
Dimitris Stamatis ~ Greece
client ~ Dimitris Stamatis

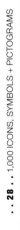

0051–0057
Cannondale Bicycle Corp. ~ USA
client ~ Cannondale Bicycle Corp.

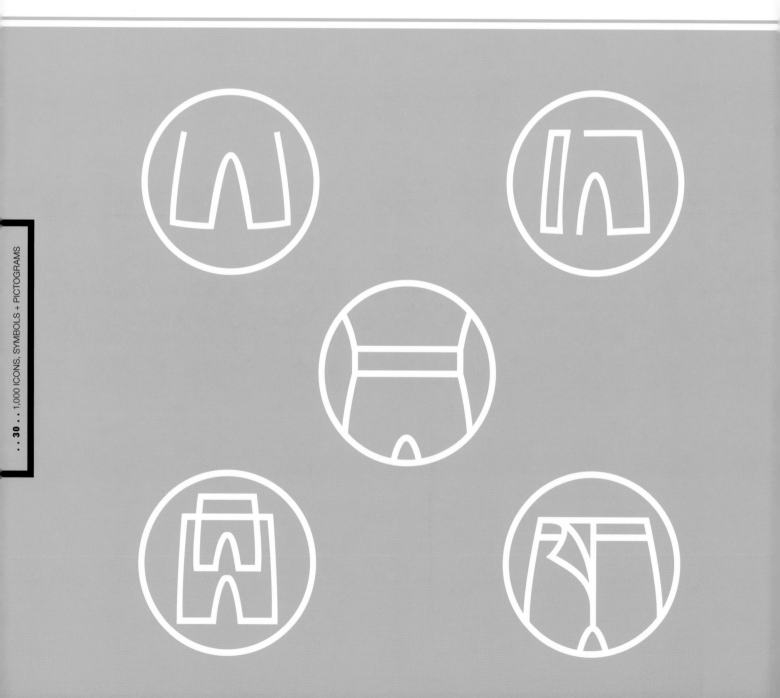

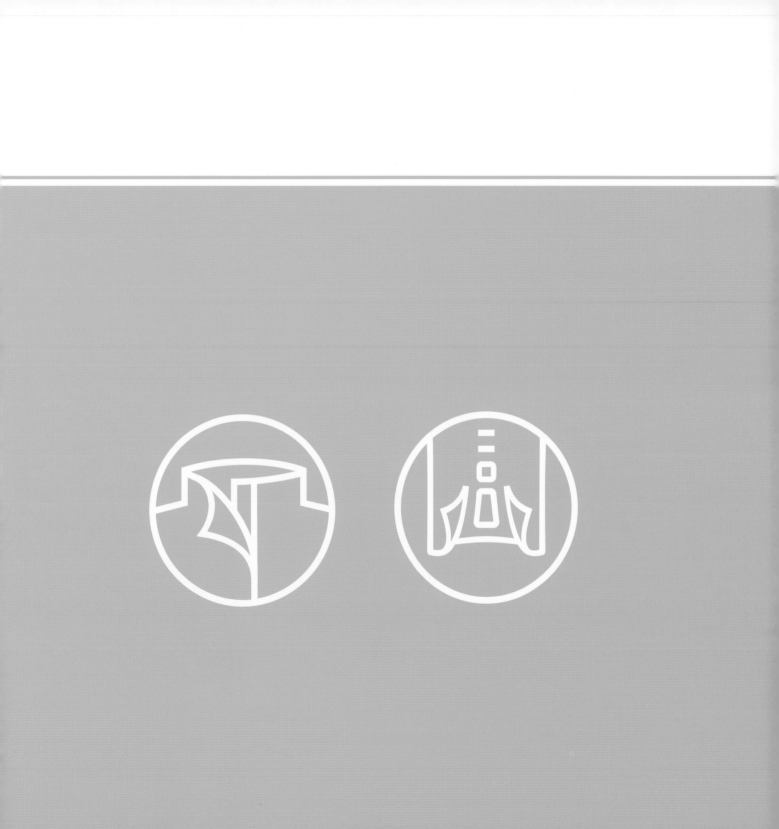

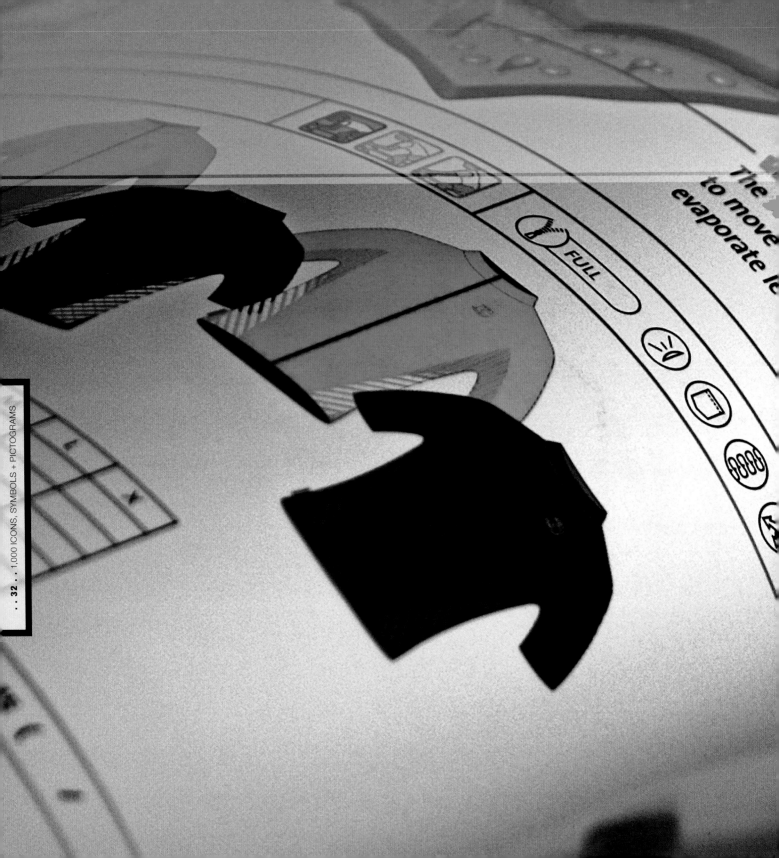

FULL

The
to move
evaporate l

Cannondale Bicycle Corp. ~ USA
client ~ Cannondale Bicycle Corp.

STRETCH
As the fabric stretches, a highly
breathable semi-mesh is created.

...llows moisture
+he body and
...ol and dry.

0058–0065
Cannondale Bicycle Corp. ~ USA
client ~ Cannondale Bicycle Corp.

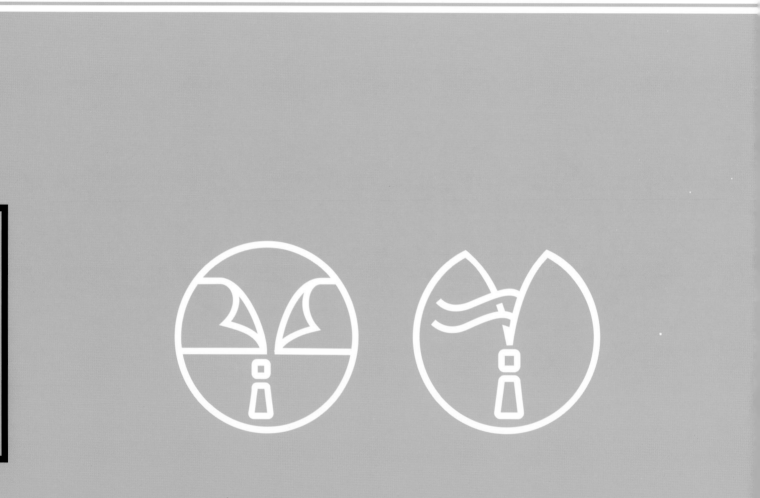

Cannondale Bicycle Corp. ~ USA
client ~ Cannondale Bicycle Corp.

ICON GUIDE

Treated to inhibit the g
bacteria

Fabric provide
harmful ult

Wi

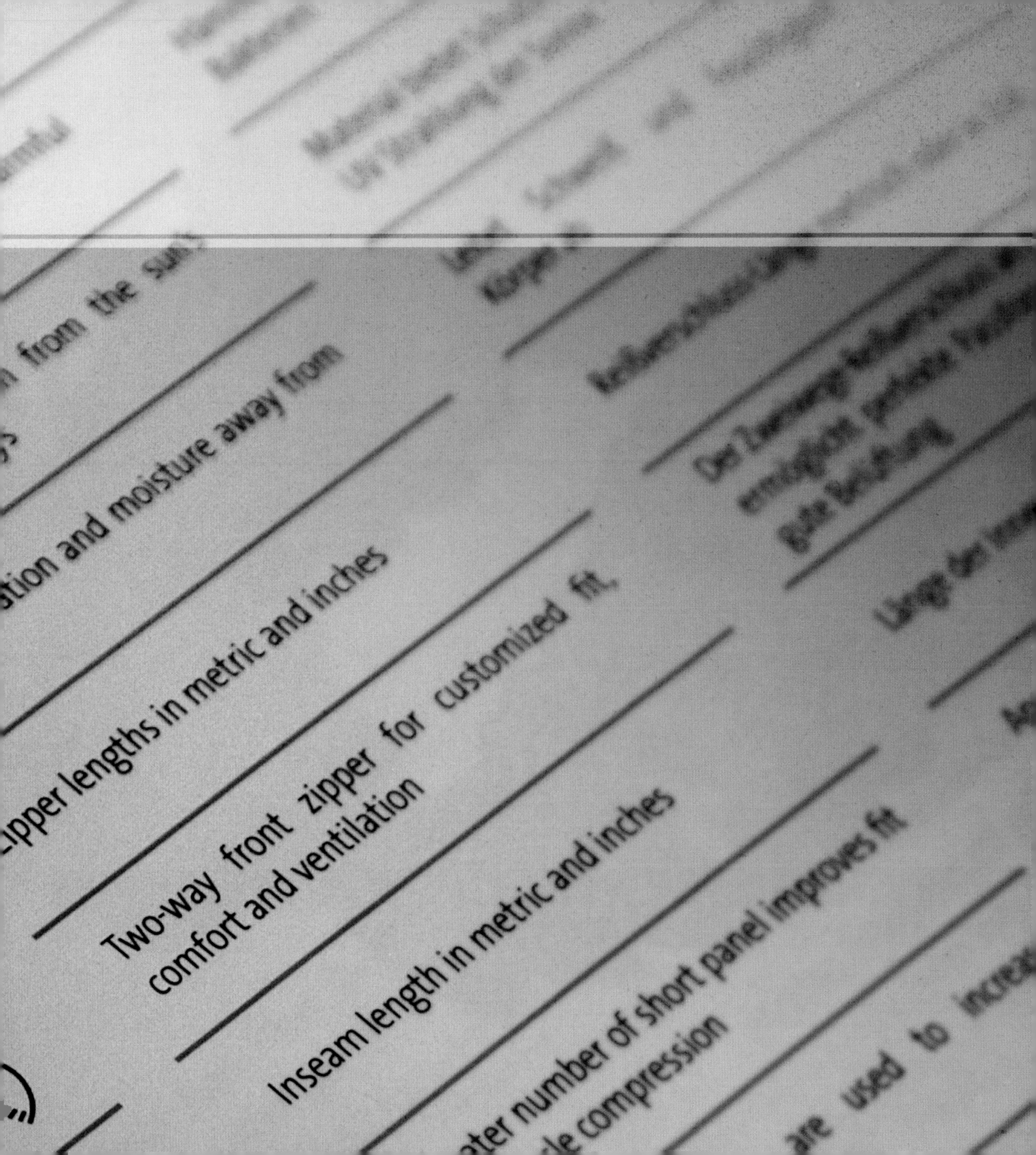

...from the sun

...tion and moisture away from

...zipper lengths in metric and inches

Two-way front zipper for customized fit, comfort and ventilation

Inseam length in metric and inches

...ter number of short panel improves fit

...le compression

...are used to increa...

0066-0075
Cannondale Bicycle Corp. ~ USA
client ~ Cannondale Bicycle Corp.

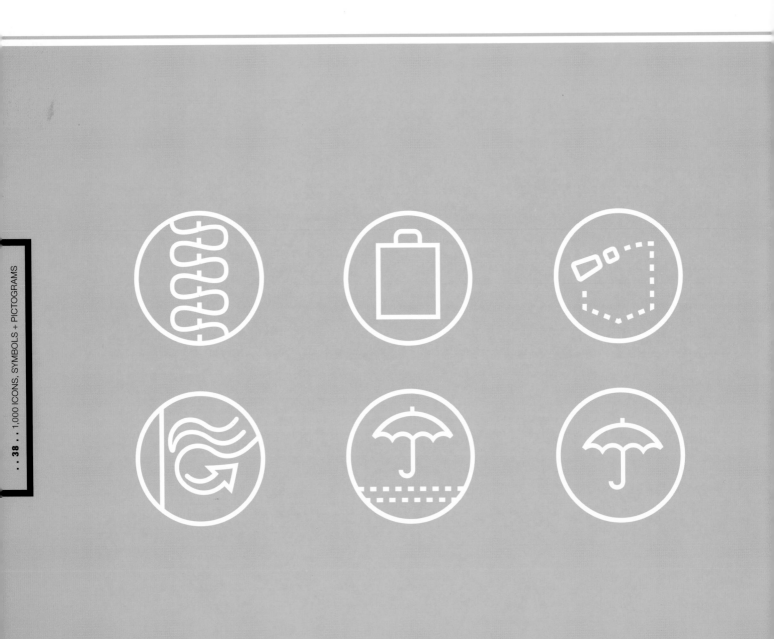

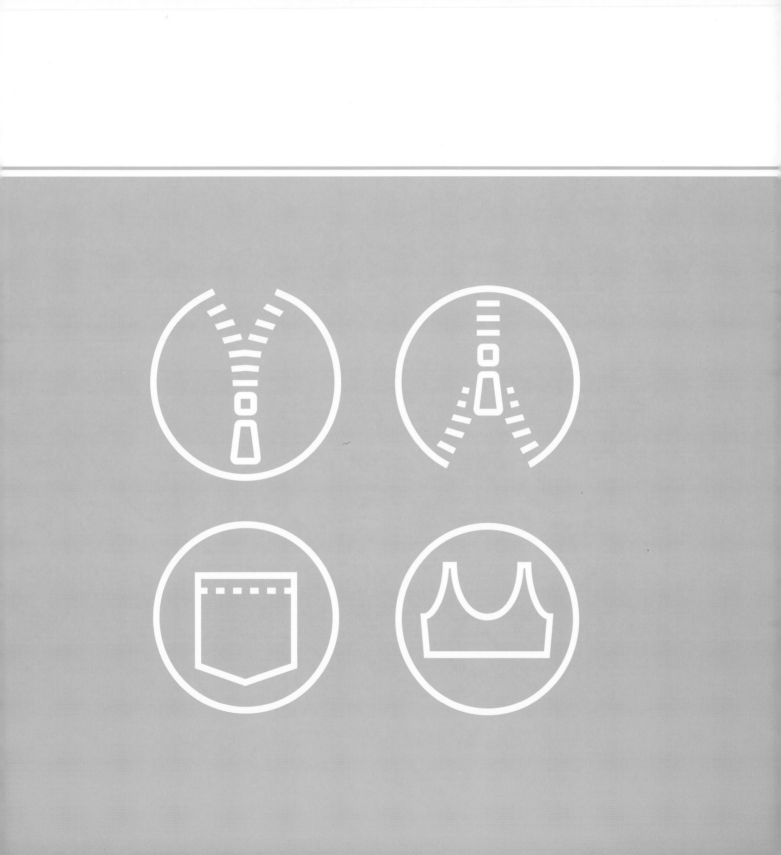

0076–0084
substance151 ~ USA
client ~ The Kitchen

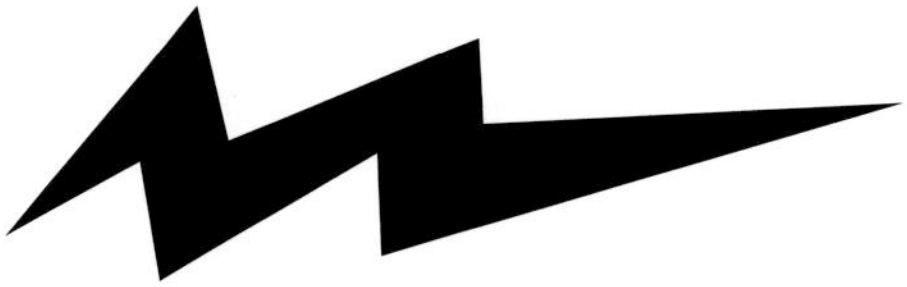

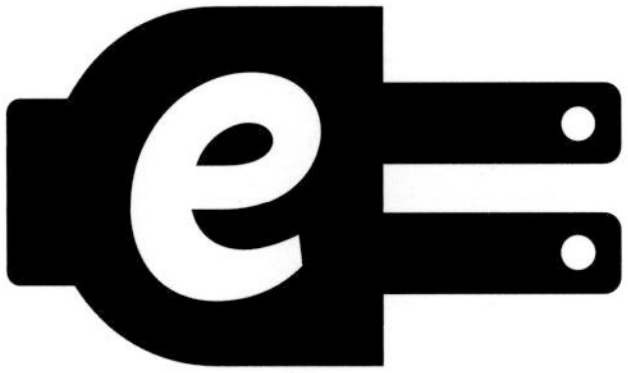

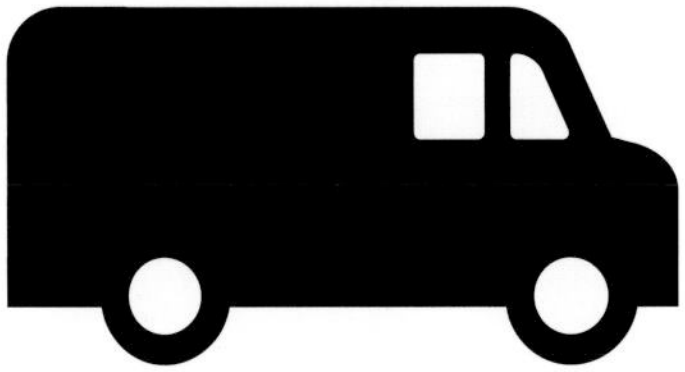

0088–0090
Cannondale Bicycle Corp. ~ USA
client ~ Cannondale Bicycle Corp.

6", 15CM

65123 PEACOCK

Cannondale Bicycle Corp. ~ USA
client ~ Cannondale Bicycle Corp.

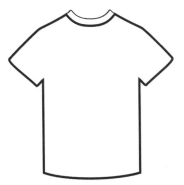

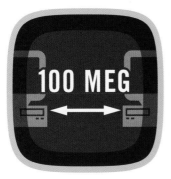

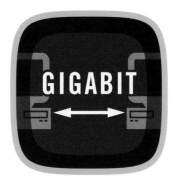

0110—0119
Kindred Design Studio ~ USA
client ~ IDX Corporation, Inc

0120—0137
Planet Propaganda ~ USA
client ~ Square Joint

. . . 52 . . . 1,000 ICONS, SYMBOLS + PICTOGRAMS

0138–0155
Planet Propaganda ~ USA
client ~ Square Joint

0156–0173
Planet Propaganda ~ USA
client ~ Square Joint

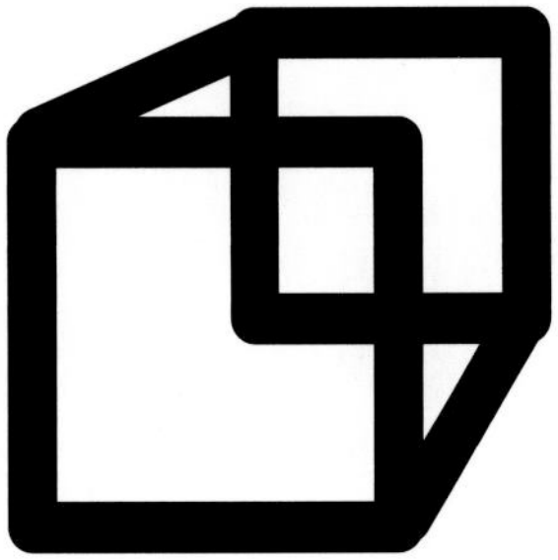

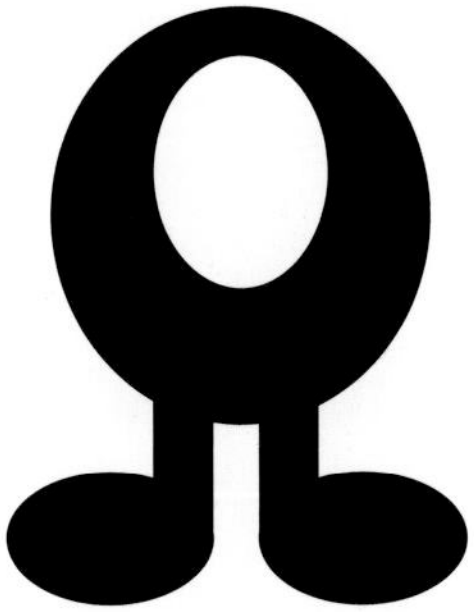

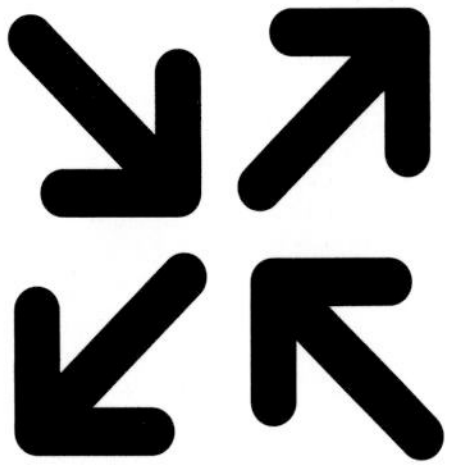

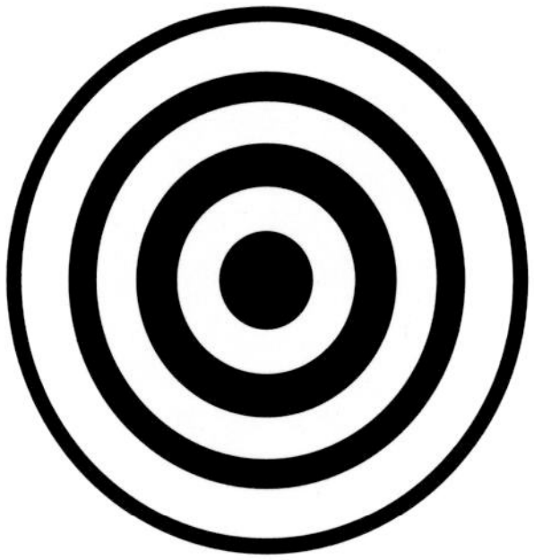

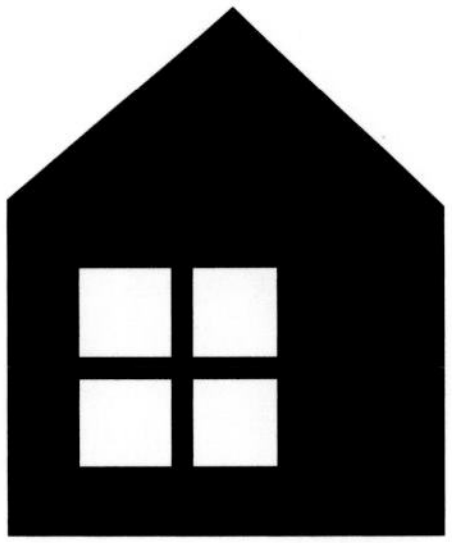

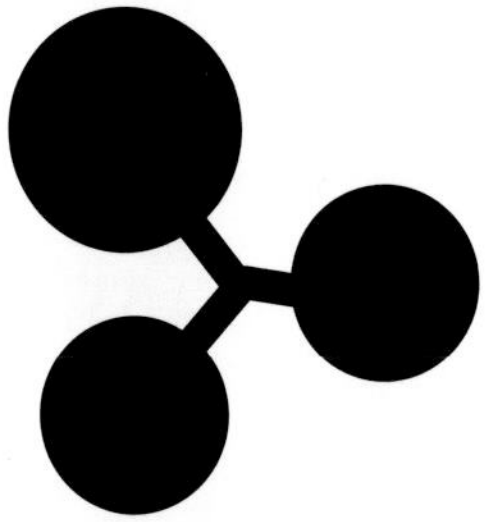

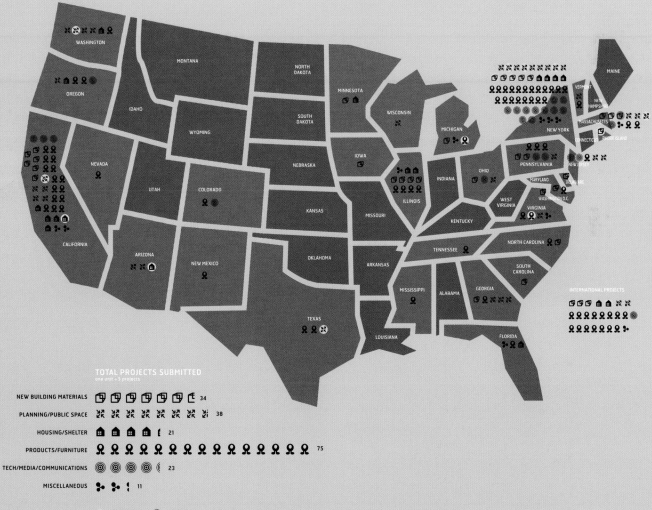

WASHINGTON

MONTANA

NORTH DAKOTA

MINNESOTA

MAINE

OREGON

IDAHO

SOUTH DAKOTA

WISCONSIN

VERMONT

NEW HAMPSHIRE

MASSACHUSETTS

WYOMING

MICHIGAN

NEW YORK

CONNECTICUT RHODE ISLAND

NEVADA

IOWA

NEBRASKA

OHIO

PENNSYLVANIA

NEW JERSEY

UTAH

COLORADO

INDIANA

ILLINOIS

MARYLAND

DELAWARE

CALIFORNIA

KANSAS

MISSOURI

WEST VIRGINIA

WASHINGTON D.C.

VIRGINIA

ARIZONA

NEW MEXICO

KENTUCKY

TENNESSEE

NORTH CAROLINA

OKLAHOMA

ARKANSAS

SOUTH CAROLINA

INTERNATIONAL PROJECTS

MISSISSIPPI

ALABAMA

GEORGIA

TEXAS

LOUISIANA

FLORIDA

TOTAL PROJECTS SUBMITTED
one unit = 5 projects

NEW BUILDING MATERIALS	34
PLANNING/PUBLIC SPACE	38
HOUSING/SHELTER	21
PRODUCTS/FURNITURE	75
TECH/MEDIA/COMMUNICATIONS	23
MISCELLANEOUS	11

= RUNNER-UP   = WINNER

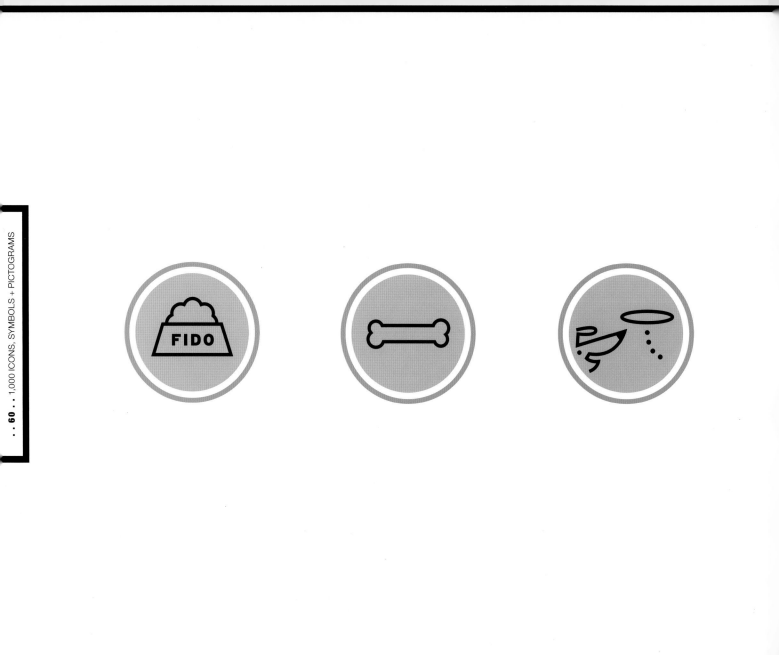

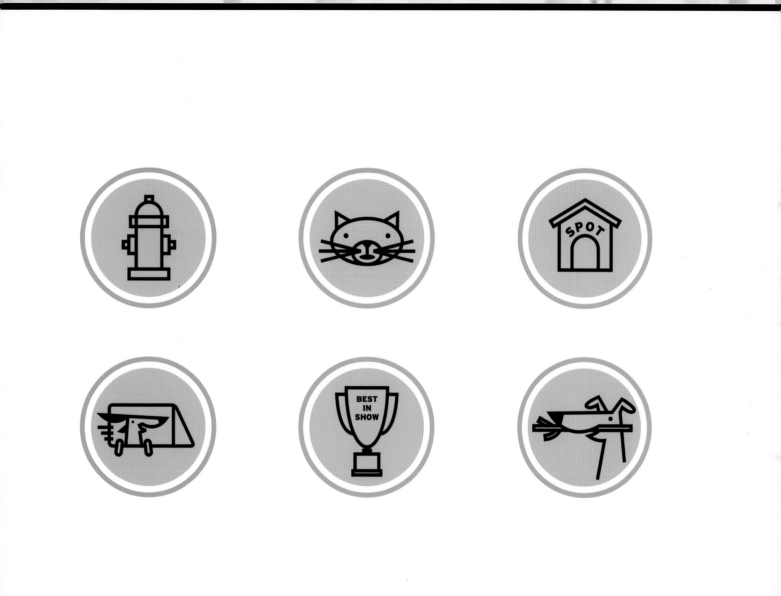

Chris Rooney Illustration/Design ~ USA
client ~ Chris Rooney

0189-0194
Chris Rooney Illustration/Design ~ USA
client ~ Chris Rooney

0195–0200
Dean Arts ~ USA
client ~ Regional Training Inst.

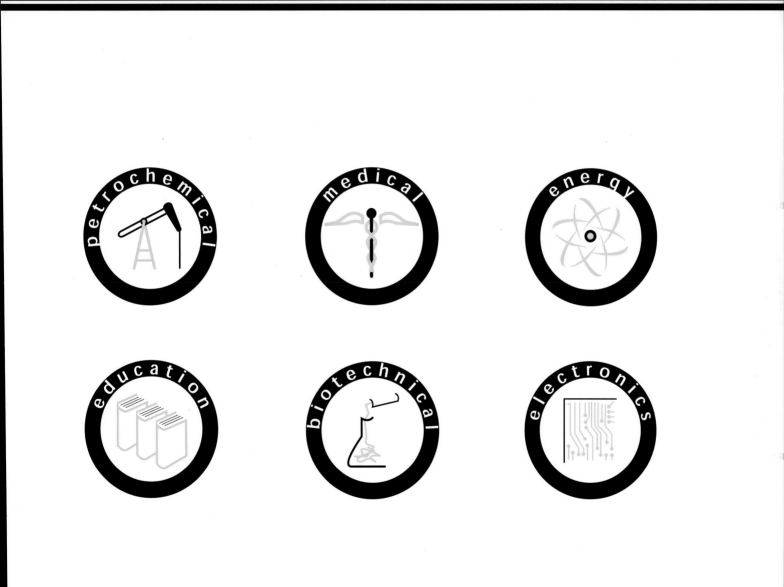

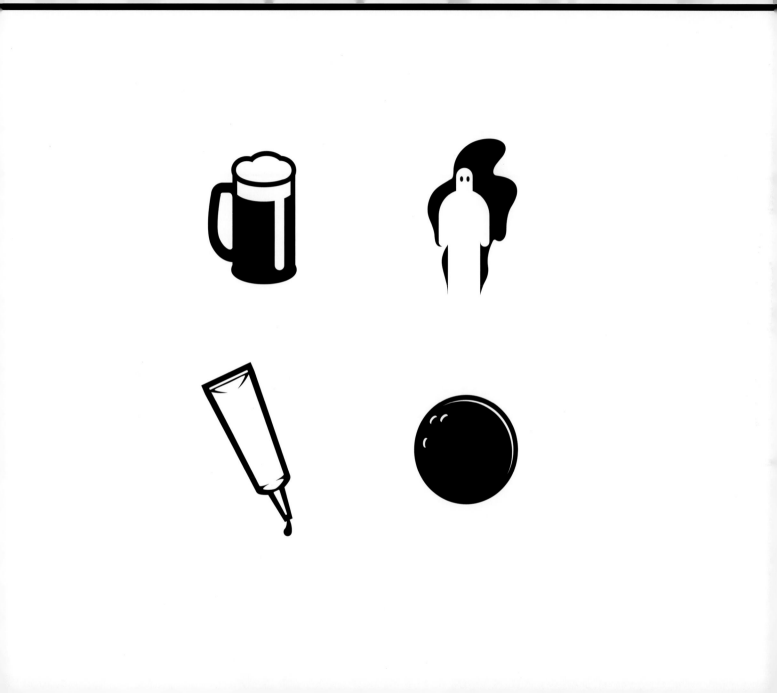

Dotzero Design ~ USA
client ~ Bridgetown Printing

0213–0214
Dresser Johnson ~ USA
client ~ Guitar World Acoustic *Magazine*

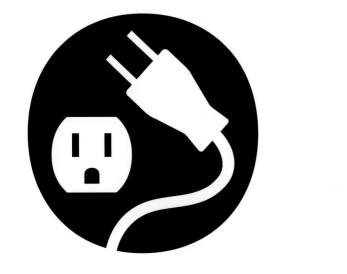

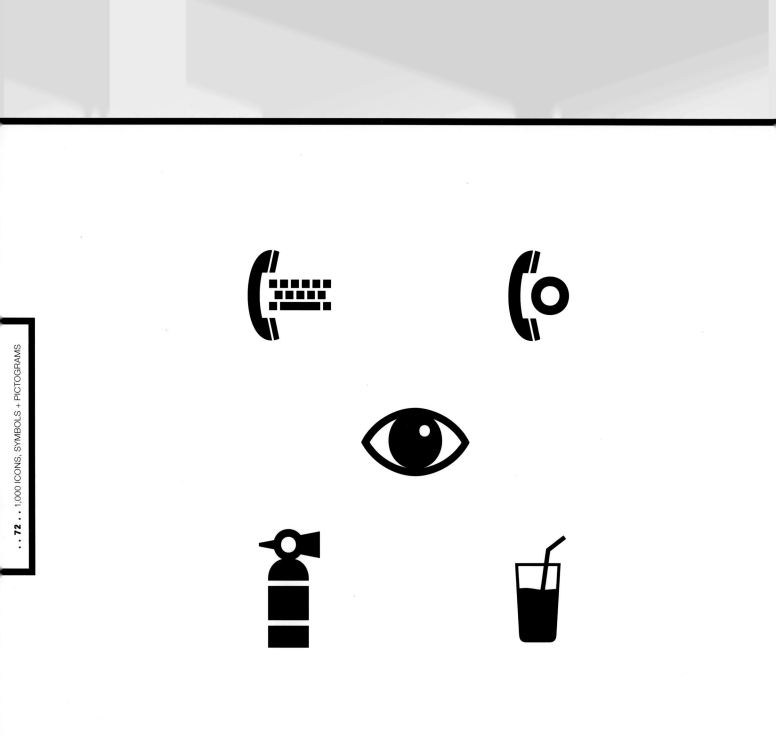

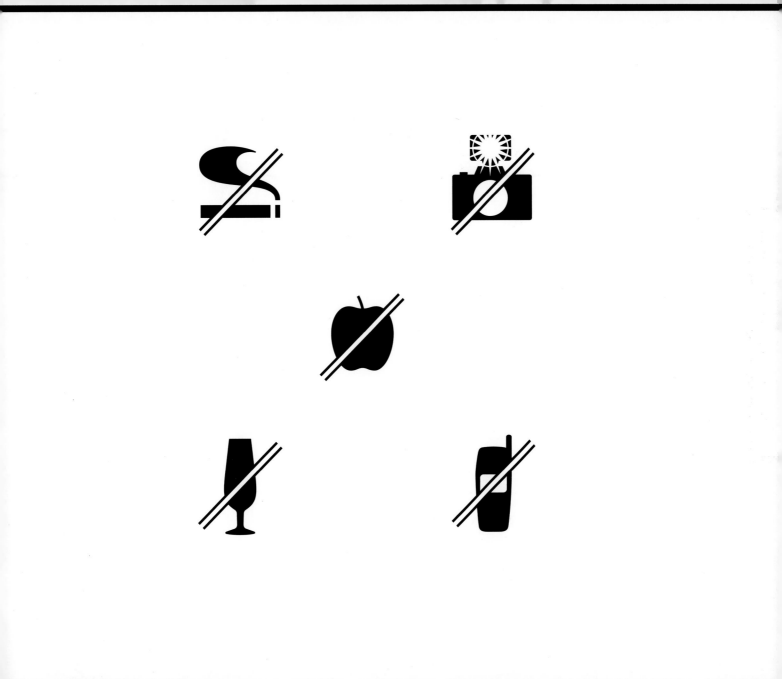

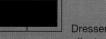

Dresser Johnson ~ USA
client ~ The Museum of Modern Art

The Museum of
11 West 53rd St

Monday
Tuesday
Wednesday
Thursday
Friday
Saturday
Sunday

ern Art

a.m. - 5:30 p.m.
d
a.m. - 5:30 p.m.
a.m. - 5:30 p.m.
a.m. - 8:00 p.m.
a.m. - 5:30 p.m.
a.m. - 5:30 p.m.

0225–0234
Dresser Johnson ~ USA
client ~ The Museum of Modern Art

. . 76 . . . 1,000 ICONS, SYMBOLS + PICTOGRAMS

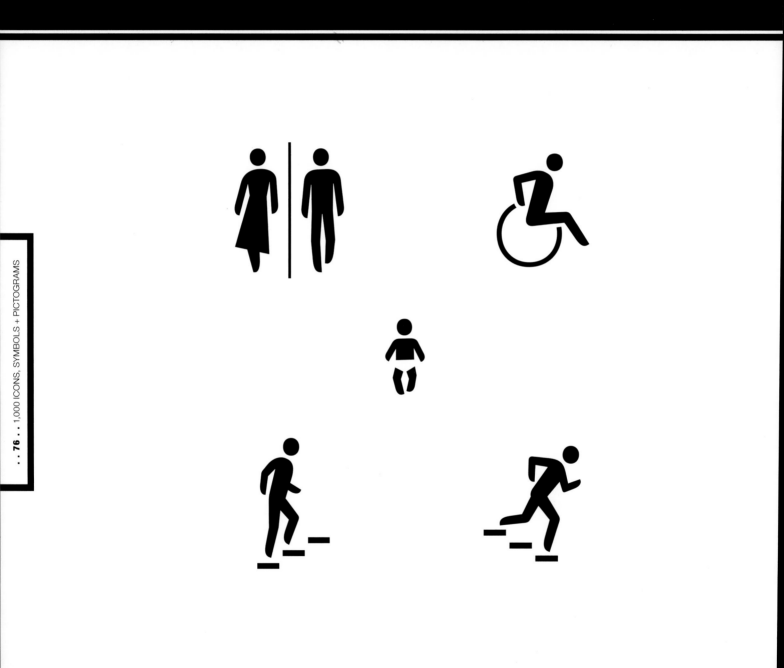

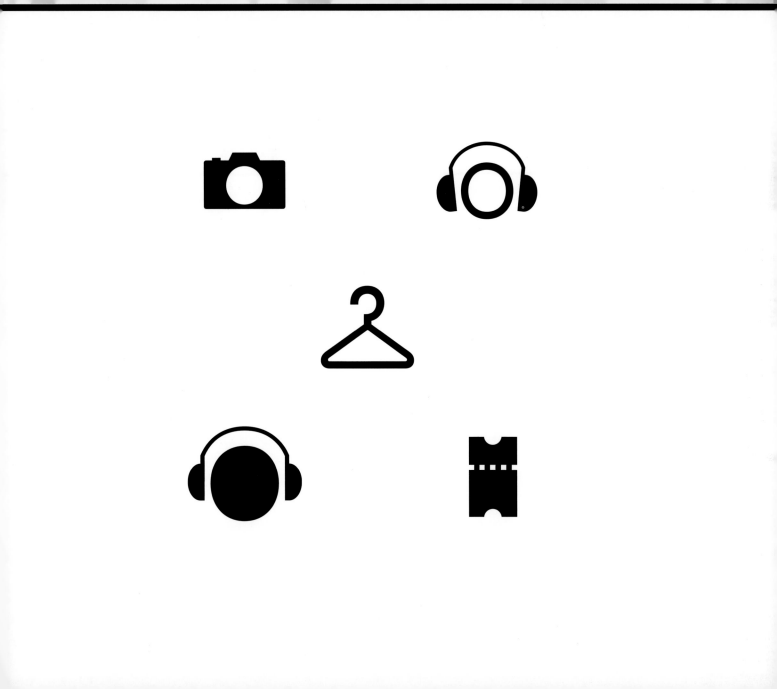

RESTROOMS

Dresser Johnson ~ USA
client ~ The Museum of Modern Art

0235-0244
GBH Design Ltd ~ UK
client ~ PUMA

. . **80** . . 1,000 ICONS, SYMBOLS + PICTOGRAMS

WISE UP

WATCH
YOUR STEP

SIZE MATTERS

MAKE ROOM
FOR OTHERS

DON'T EAT
RUBBISH

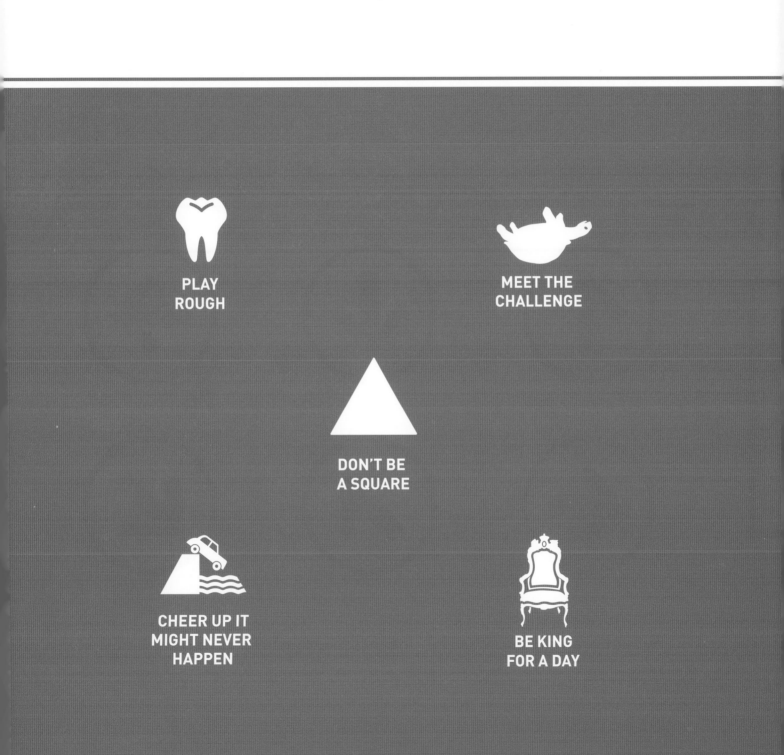

PLAY
ROUGH

MEET THE
CHALLENGE

DON'T BE
A SQUARE

CHEER UP IT
MIGHT NEVER
HAPPEN

BE KING
FOR A DAY

0245–0256
Federico Panzano ~ Italy
client ~ Hospital E.O. "Ospedali Galliera"

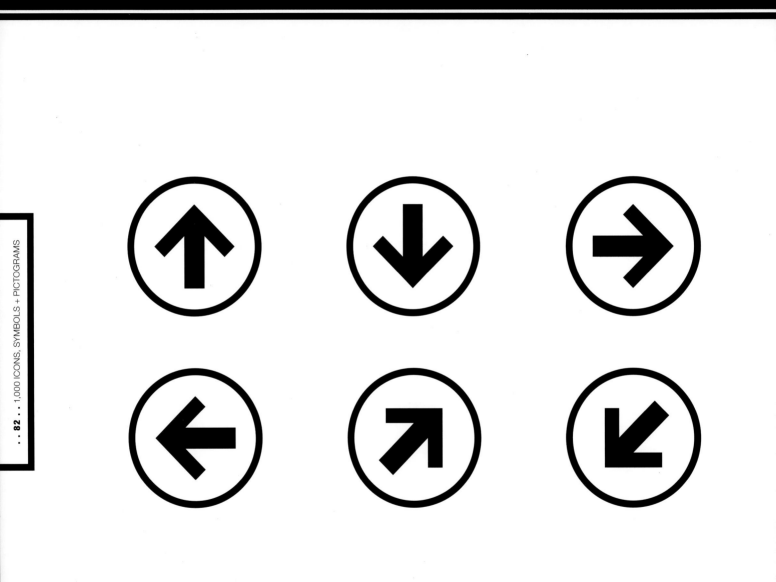

Federico Panzano ~ Italy
client ~ Hospital E.O. "Ospedali Galliera"

pital Signage System
"Ospedali Galliera" - Genoa, Italy

0257–0268
Federico Panzano ~ Italy
client ~ Hospital E.O. "Ospedali Galliera"

0281-0286
Federico Panzano ~ Italy
client ~ Hospital E.O. "Ospedali Galliera"

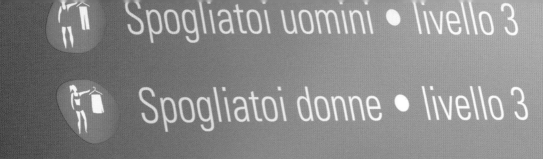

Spogliatoi uomini • livello 3

Spogliatoi donne • livello 3

Thermæ

Beauty Center • livello 1

Idromassaggio • livello 3

Tepidarium • livello 3

Vasca termale • livello 3

Percorso Kneipp • livello 3

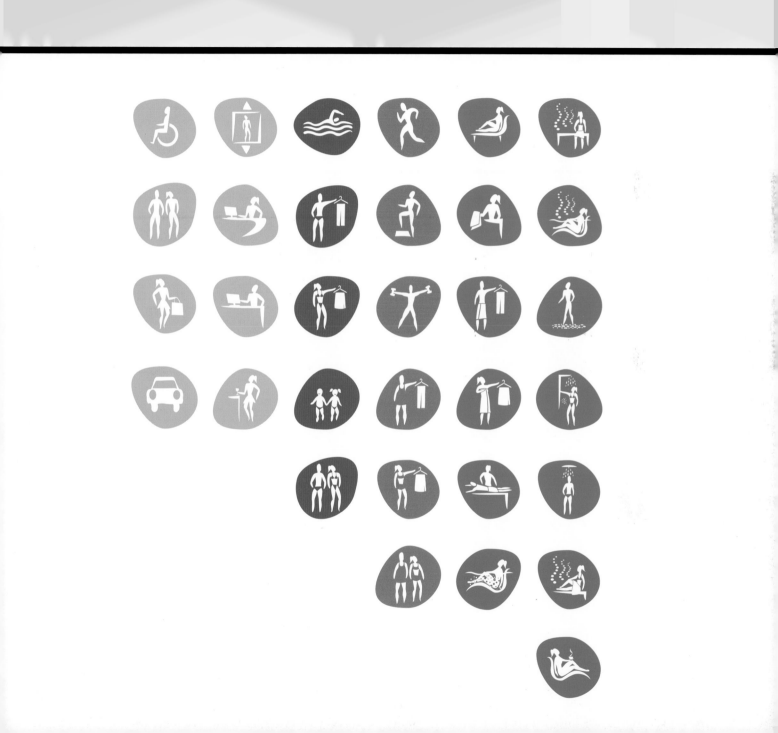

0331-0337
Blackcoffee ~ USA
client ~ Naked Lion Brewing Company

Blackcoffee ~ USA
client ~ Naked Lion Brewing Company

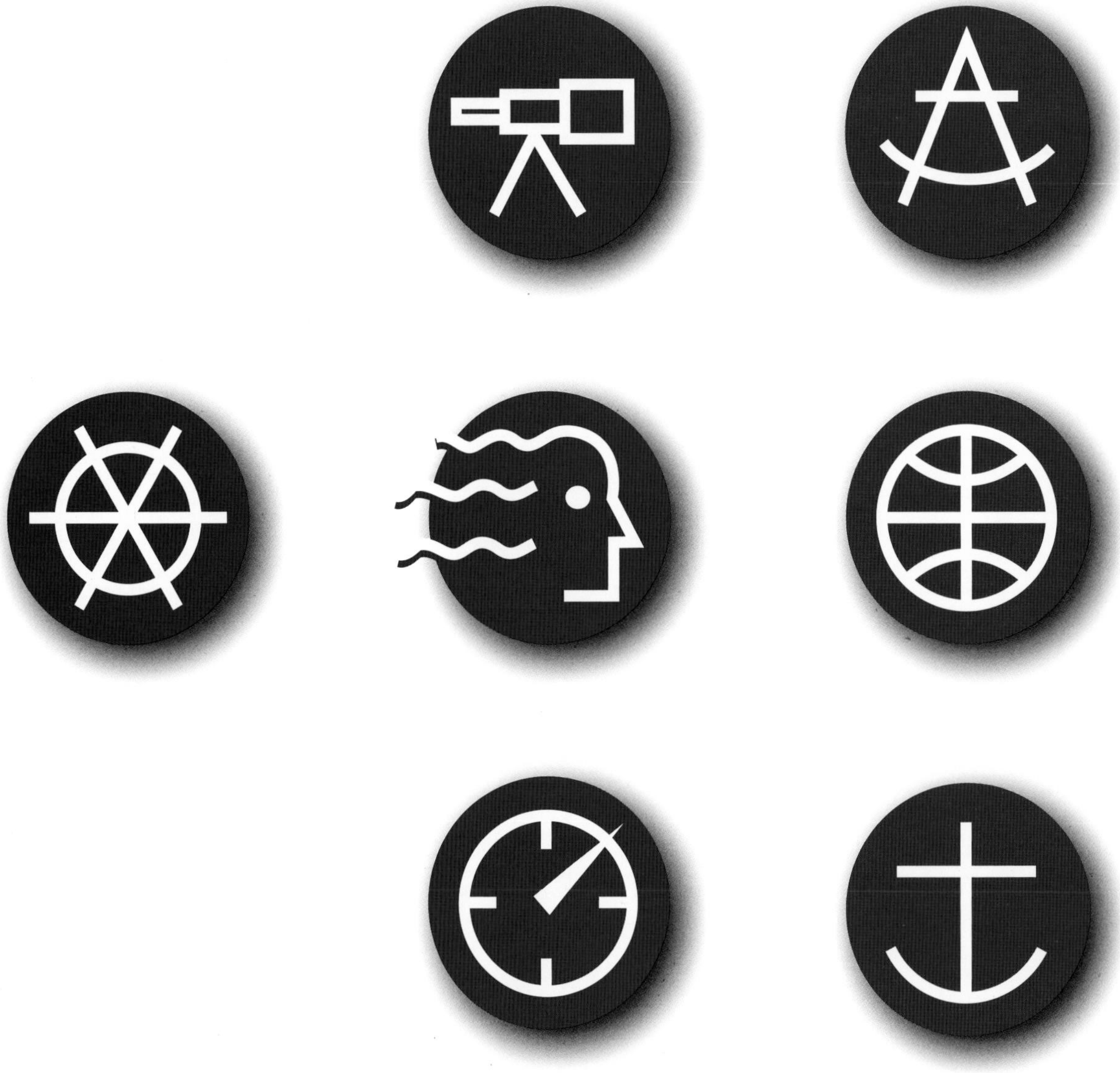

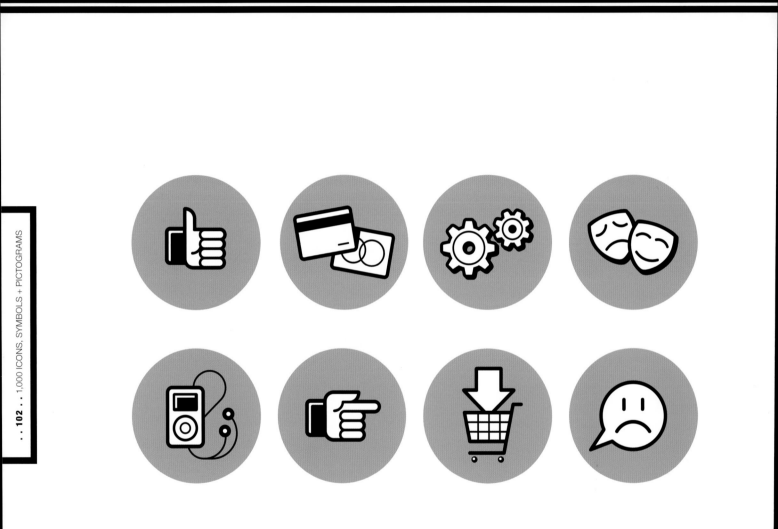

0361–0376
Glitschka Studios ~ USA
client ~ Glitschka Studios

0377–0384
Glitschka Studios ~ USA
client ~ Glitschka Studios

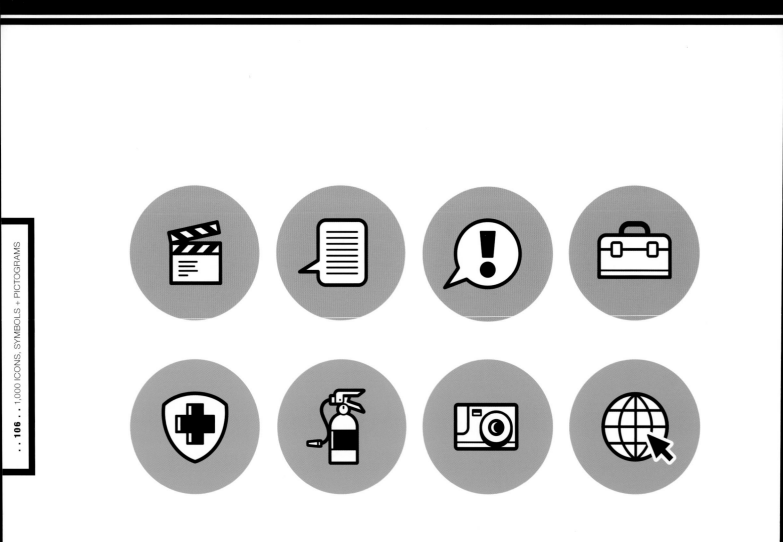

0385-0387
Sayles Graphic Design ~ USA
client ~ IshopDesMoines.com

I SHOP DESMOINES.COM

921 40TH STREET
WEST DES MO

Sayles Graphic Design ~ USA
client ~ IshopDesMoines.com

nightlife

dining

shopping

(515) 681-SHOP

0388–0391
The-Groop ~ USA
client ~ The-Groop

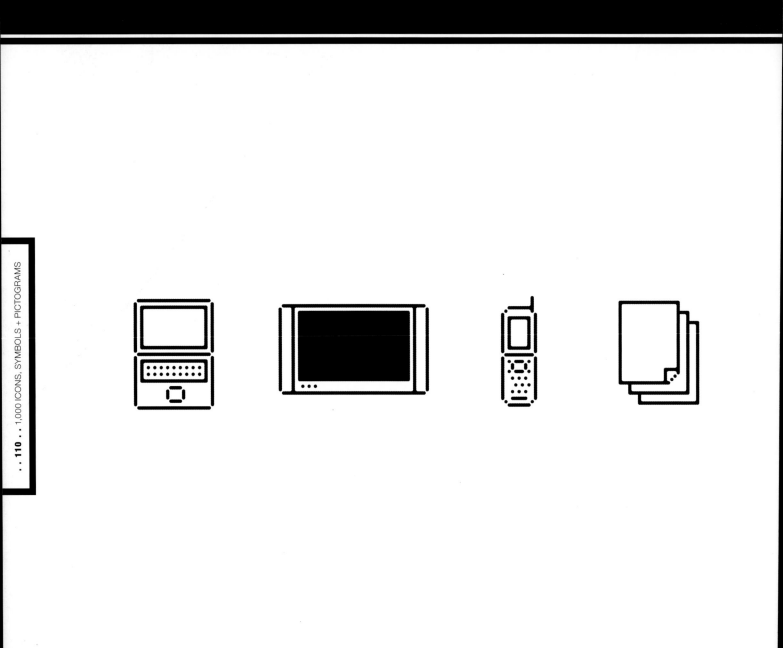

. . **110** . . 1,000 ICONS, SYMBOLS + PICTOGRAMS

PC TV MOBILE PRINT

Expanding your business: now and in the future. Different industries discover product benefits in different ways.

FULLPRESS, WEBNATIVE & WEBNATIVE VENTURE: INNOVATIVE SOLUTIONS FOR COMPETITIVE MARKETS

XINET'S SCALABLE SOLUTIONS GROW WITH YOUR BUSINESS, SPEEDING LOCAL AND REMOTE PRODUCTION — ACROSS THE OFFICE AND AROUND THE WORLD.

FullPress® server software alleviates the bottlenecks that businesses encounter when they work with large image files. With FullPress at the center of the workflow, managing file-sharing, minimizing network traffic, and sending output to any device on the network, sites can speed production, reduce costs and increase output.

Adding *WebNative*™ to the FullPress workflow extends services over the Internet, giving customers, staff and collaborative partners instant access to digital assets. In addition to the advantages of centralized multi-site asset sharing, WebNative also streamlines many production

archiving and restoring. WebNative is an incredibly versatile system that can be used for corporate brand management, as well as creating new Web-enabled production workflows.

Xinet's *WebNative* ™ *Venture* combines all of the functionality and ease-of-use of WebNative with an enterprise-strength SQL database—for even faster searching, organizing, and categorizing of data—creating an asset-management system that's completely and automatically integrated into each site's existing FullPress workflow.

Gee + Chung Design ~ USA
client ~ Xinet, Inc

0392–0431
Gee + Chung Design ~ USA
client ~ Xinet, Inc

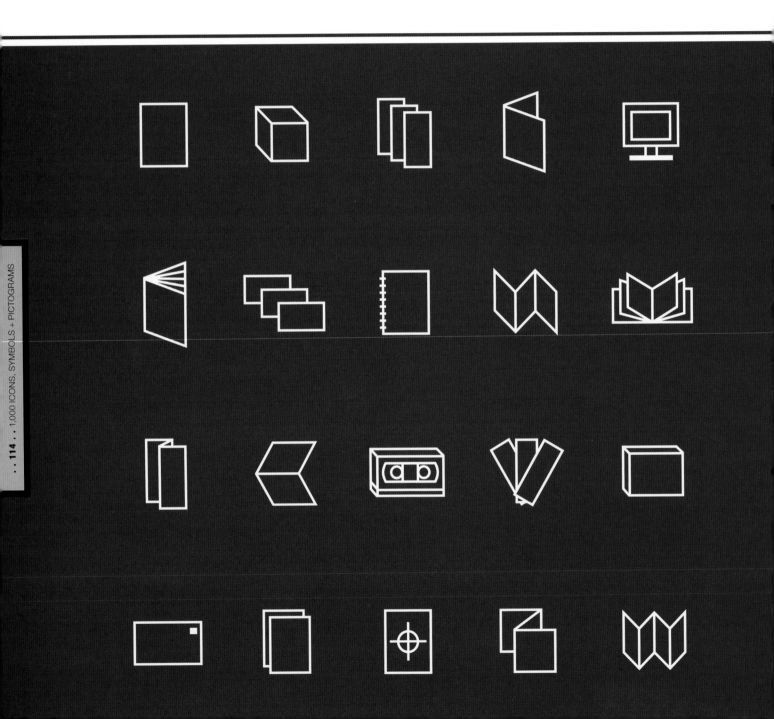

Gee + Chung Design ~ USA
client ~ Xinet, Inc

0432–0461
Gee + Chung Design ~ USA
client ~ Xinet, Inc

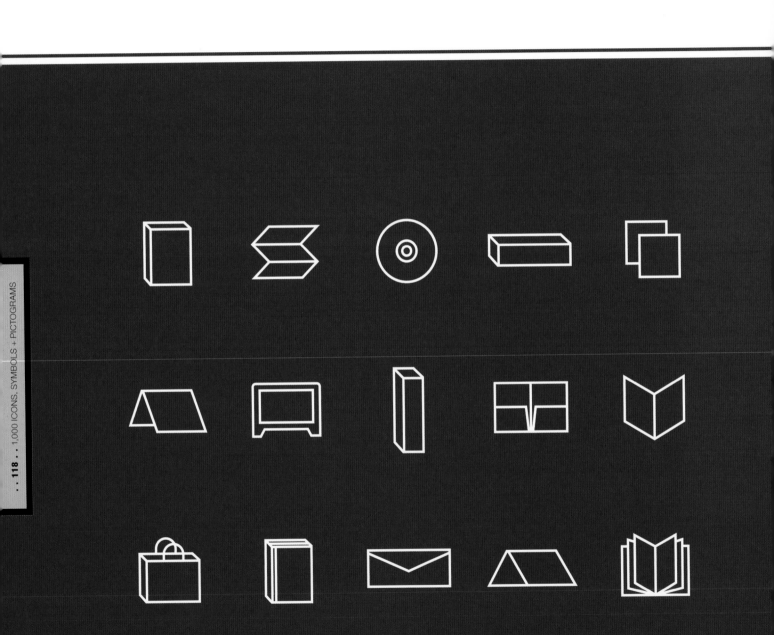

0462–0479
LSD ~ Spain
client ~ URIC Rey Juan Carlos University

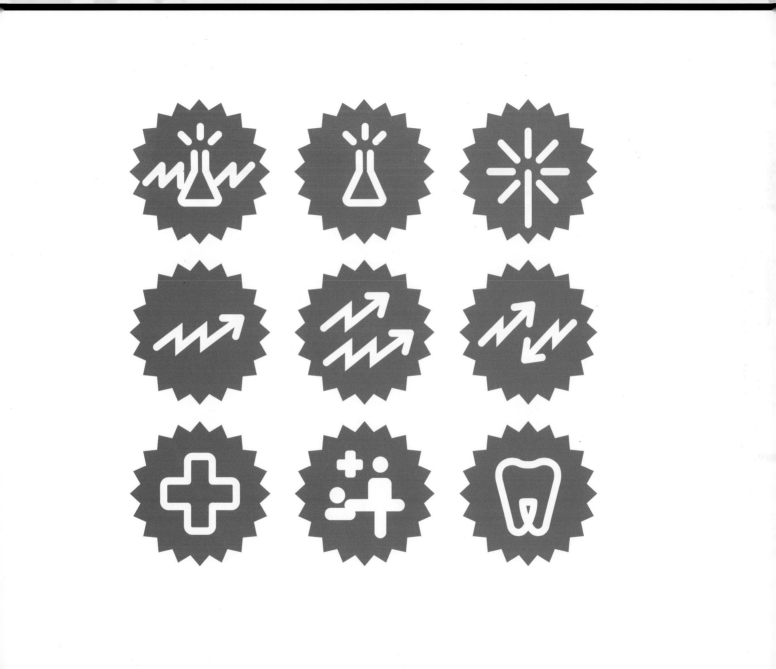

Inpraxis, Kommunikation + Design ~ Germany
client ~ Inpraxis, Kommunikation + Design

inpraxis::

Syntegral Design Strategie
Der gemeinsame Weg

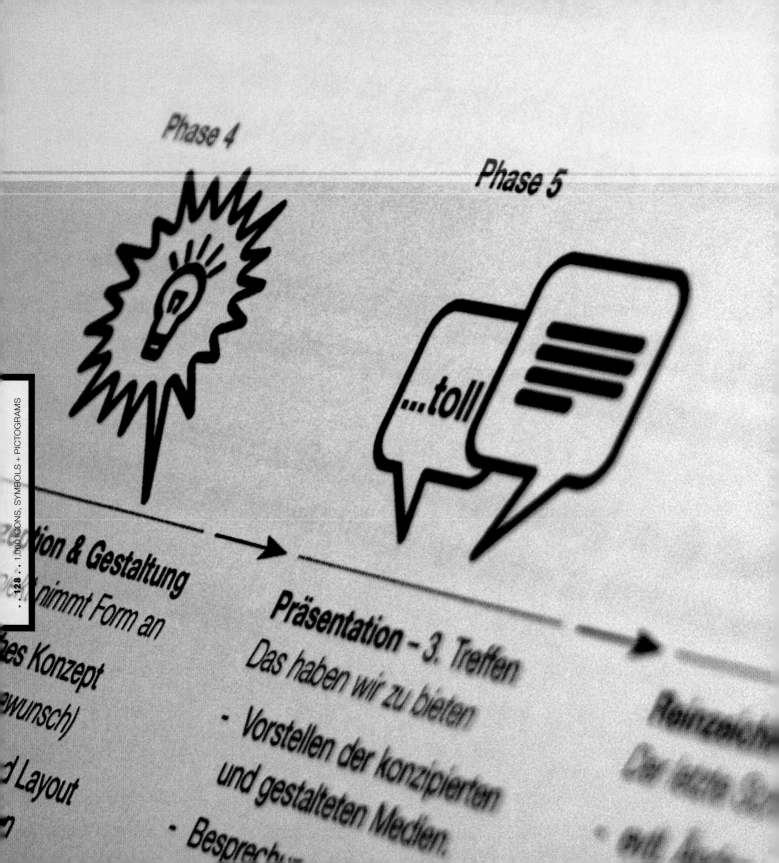

Inpraxis, Kommunikation + Design ~ Germany
client ~ Inpraxis, Kommunikation + Design

0500-0505
studiovertex ~ USA
client ~ PetroCard

. . **130** . . 1,000 ICONS, SYMBOLS + PICTOGRAMS

...ATE ONE CAR, SEVERAL
...N A FLEET OF TRUCKS, PETROCARD
...CLOSELY WITH YOU TO DEVELOP A
...ZED FUEL MANAGEMENT PROGRAM THAT
...UR COMPANY, FLEET AND BUDGET.

...CARD PROVIDES DETAILED REPORTING,
...TITIVE PRICES AND REDUCED PAPERWORK.
...- SAVE TIME, MONEY AND BE ABLE TO MANAGE
...FUEL PROGRAM MORE EFFECTIVELY.

...MORE THAN 30 YEARS EXPERIENCE IN THE
...OLEUM INDUSTRY, PETROCARD IS THE LEADER
...ARDLOCK AND MOBILE FUELING,

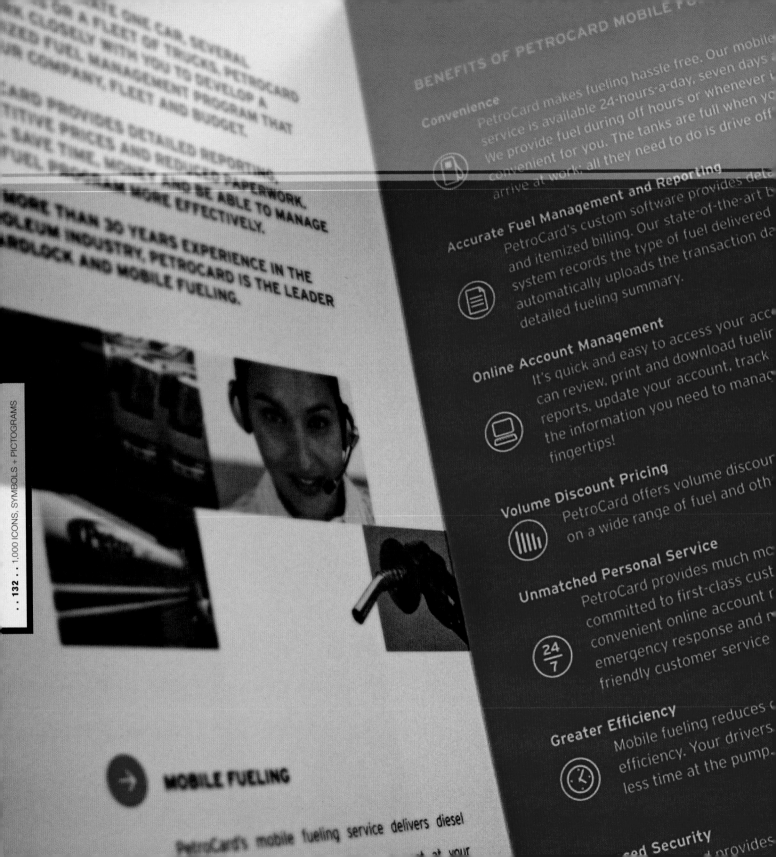

→ **MOBILE FUELING**

PetroCard's mobile fueling service delivers diesel
...t at your

BENEFITS OF PETROCARD MOBILE FU...

Convenience
PetroCard makes fueling hassle free. Our mobile
service is available 24-hours-a-day, seven days
We provide fuel during off hours or whenever i
convenient for you. The tanks are full when yo
arrive at work; all they need to do is drive off

Accurate Fuel Management and Reporting
PetroCard's custom software provides deta
and itemized billing. Our state-of-the-art b
system records the type of fuel delivered
automatically uploads the transaction da
detailed fueling summary.

Online Account Management
It's quick and easy to access your acc
can review, print and download fuelir
reports, update your account, track
the information you need to manac
fingertips!

Volume Discount Pricing
PetroCard offers volume discour
on a wide range of fuel and oth

Unmatched Personal Service
PetroCard provides much mo
committed to first-class cust
convenient online account r
emergency response and r
friendly customer service

Greater Efficiency
Mobile fueling reduces
efficiency. Your drivers
less time at the pump.

...ed Security
...d provides

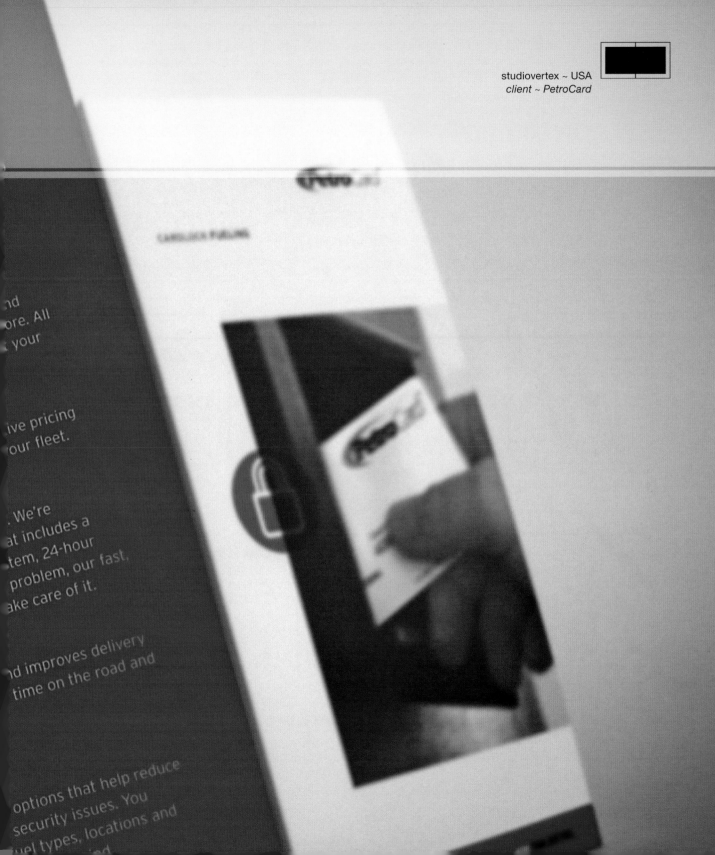

studiovertex ~ USA
client ~ PetroCard

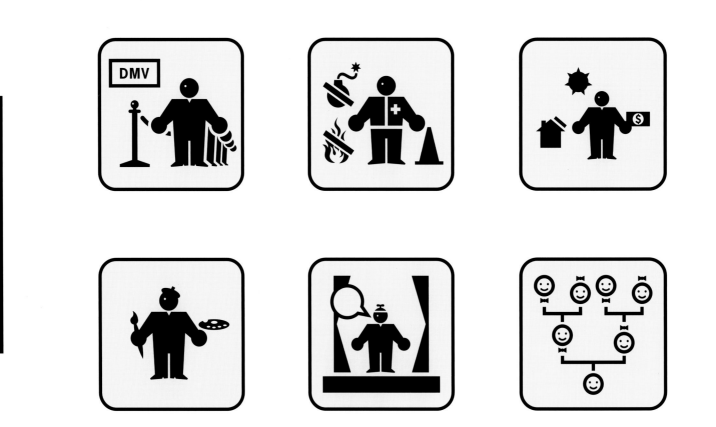

ic Info

Police: 911
1 Hamilton Dr. Mill Valley
Information calls only: 415/389-4100
Fire Department: 911
1 Hamilton Dr. Mill Valley
Information calls only: 415/389-4130
Parks & Recreation
180 Camino Alto, Mill Valley
415/383-1370

all
Ave.
94939
0; fax: 415/927-5022
: Jean Bonander
(meets 1st & 3rd Wednesday
th, 7:30 pm)

ner
nctot
. Lubamersky
ndstrom
: 400 Magnolia Ave. Larkspur
927-5005
Department: 911
Doherty Dr. Larkspur
emergencies: 415/927-5150
Department: 911
dept. information: 415/927-5110
creation information: 415/927-6746

MILL VALLEY

NOVATO

Novato City Hall
900 Sherman Ave.
Novato, CA 94945
415/897-4311; fax: 415/897-4354
City Manager: Roderick Wood
City Council (meets 2nd & 4th Tuesday of
each month, 7pm)
Mike Di Giorgio
Carole Dillon-Knutson
Pat Eklund
Bernard Meyers
John Mani
Library: 1720 Novato Blvd., Novato
415/897-1141
Police Department: 911
909 Machin Ave., Novato
Non-emergencies: 415/897-4361
Department—911
Blvd. Novato

Chris Rooney Illustration/Design ~ USA
client ~ Pacific Sun

"It'll make it all worth it if just one of you benefits from the wisdom that grew out of my vehicular woes."

Tips for dealing with traffic court and the DMV

There were times over the past few years when I wanted to drive my shiny, little, red Escort to the top of the highest hill around, put it in neutral and let it roll down the bay—just so I wouldn't have to deal anymore. Those moments were during two years of my life that I successfully register my car in ... through the hoops ... of Vehicles, Marin ... Three

requested over the phone), make appoin... ments (which seriously cut down your ... time and can also be made by phone) ... sample driver's license tests, renew ... istration, purchase personalized pl... directions to DMV offices, link ... mative Web sites and more. In ... Marinites should also be able ... site to find out up-to-the-m... at Corte Madera and No... already possible to find ... Francisco, Oakland an... In addition to pr... ral informatio...

DON'T BE A BOILED FROG

A PRACTICAL GUIDE
to Brand Building in a Dot.Com World

0518-0523

Chris Rooney Illustration/Design ~ USA

client ~ Young & Rubicam

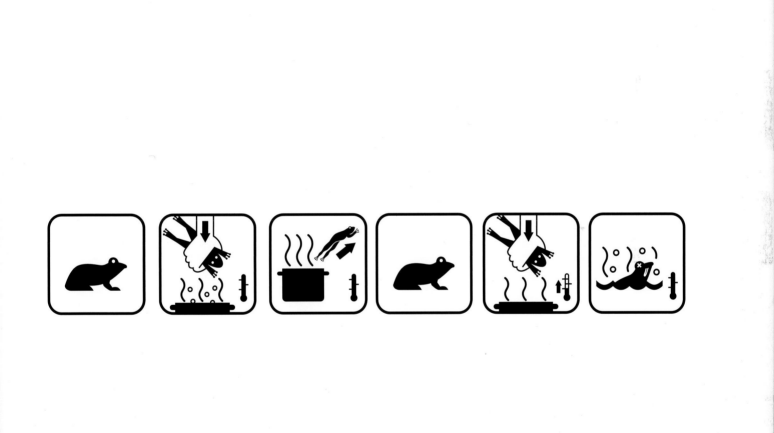

0524–0528
substance151 ~ USA
client ~ LightWorks

. . **140** . . . 1,000 ICONS, SYMBOLS + PICTOGRAMS

0529-0534
TnTom Design ~ USA
client ~ HOW *Magazine*

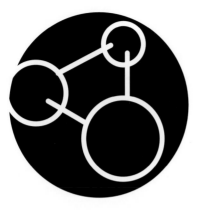

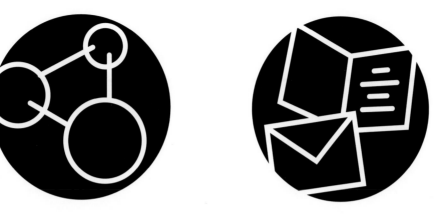

TnTom Design ~ USA
client ~ HOW *Magazine*

BESTOFSI

Seeking balance

San Francisc

to win the

life and work, t

gner crafted a promotion

ts of her dreams, by Megan Lane

0535-0542
TnTom Design ~ USA
client ~ HOW *Magazine*

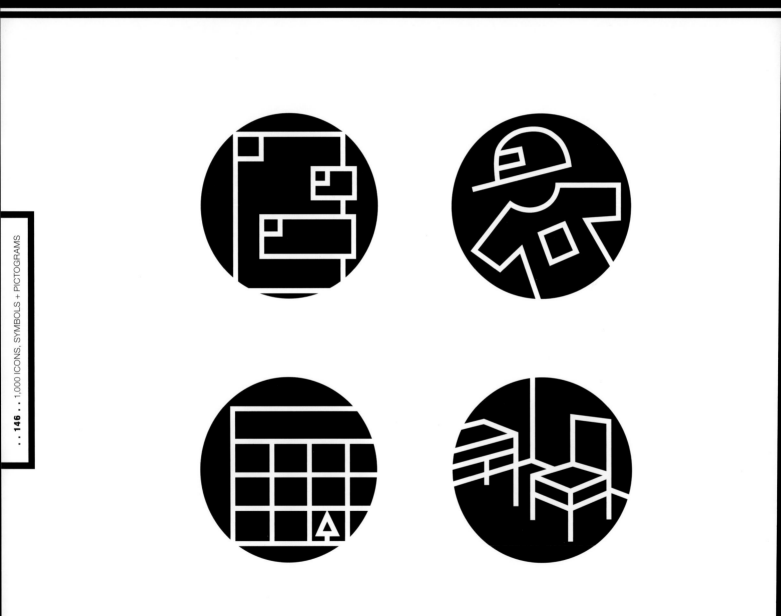

TnTom Design ~ USA
client ~ HOW Magazine

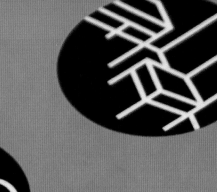

Tom, Augusta GA; (706) 495-8664

0543-0562
Muggie Ramadani Design Studio ~ Denmark
client ~ Blumoller A/S

. . 150 . . 1,000 ICONS, SYMBOLS + PICTOGRAMS

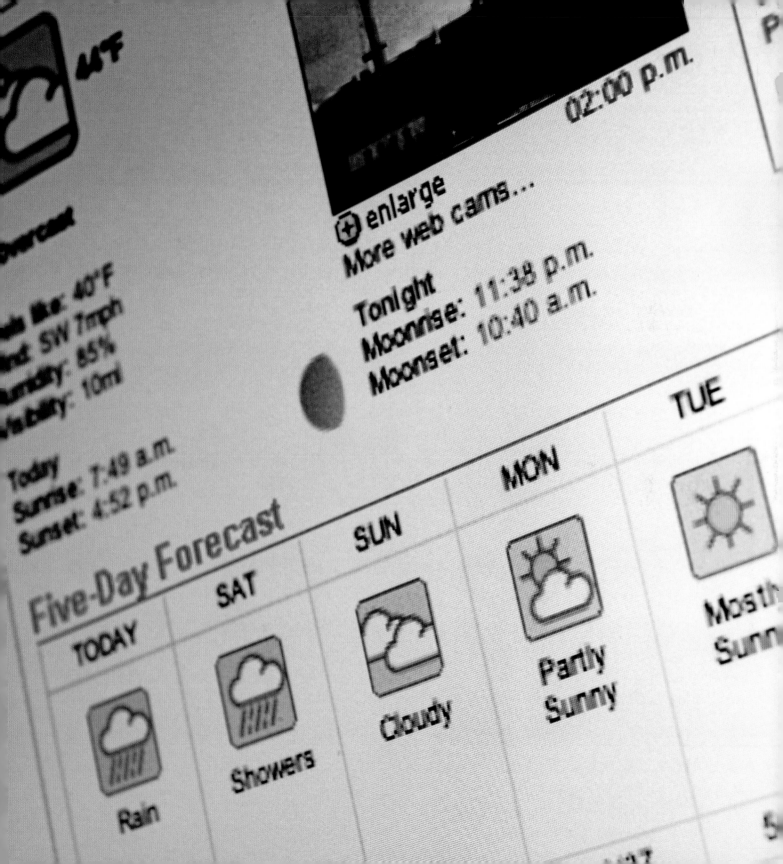

0572
Blackcoffee ~ USA
client ~ SBR

0573–0574
Blackcoffee ~ USA
client ~ Blackcoffee

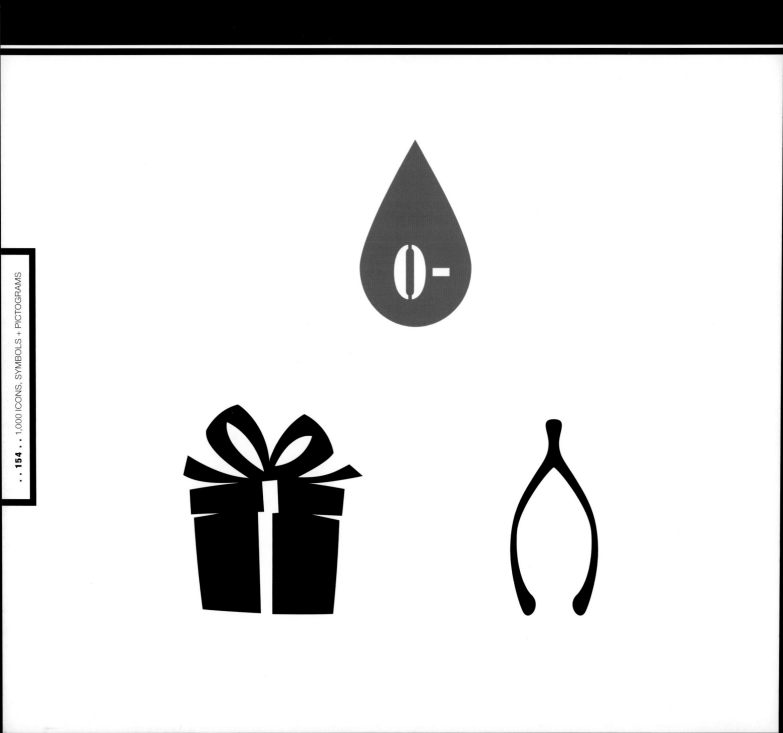

fee
$4 parking
▼

free bus ride
▼

picnic

addysha

ke chabot municipal golf co

$26/hoofing the whole 18 holes

$39/lazily joyriding the 18 holes

▼

Chris Rooney Illustration/Design ~ USA
client ~ Young & Rubicam

four

mber nineteenth

ke chabot

0575—0583
Chris Rooney Illustration/Design ~ USA
client ~ Young & Rubicam

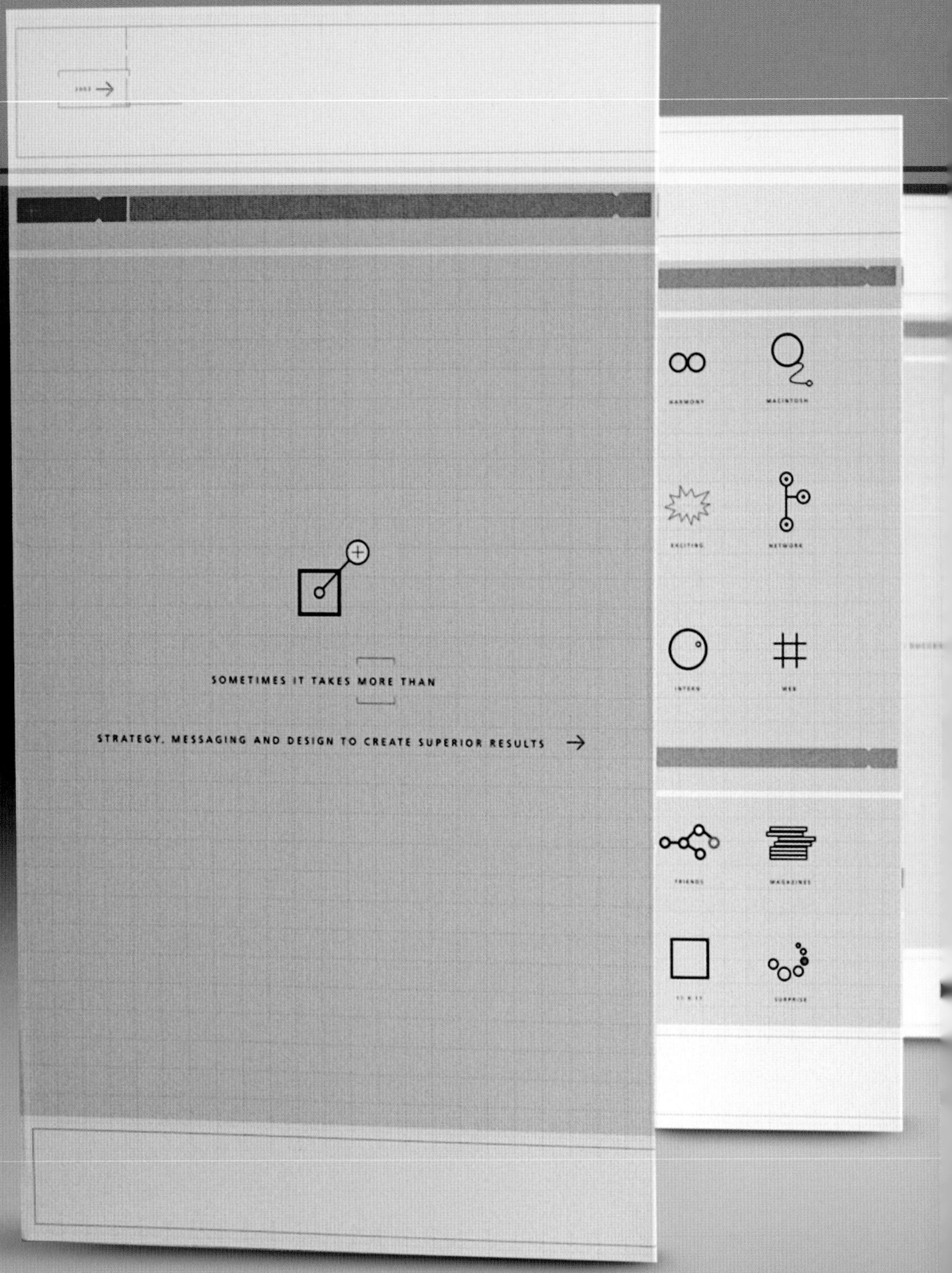

SOMETIMES IT TAKES MORE THAN

STRATEGY, MESSAGING AND DESIGN TO CREATE SUPERIOR RESULTS →

HARMONY   MACINTOSH

EXCITING   NETWORK

INTERN   WEB

FRIENDS   MAGAZINES

SURPRISE

Belyea ~ USA
client ~ Belyea

0584—0595
Belyea ~ USA
client ~ Belyea

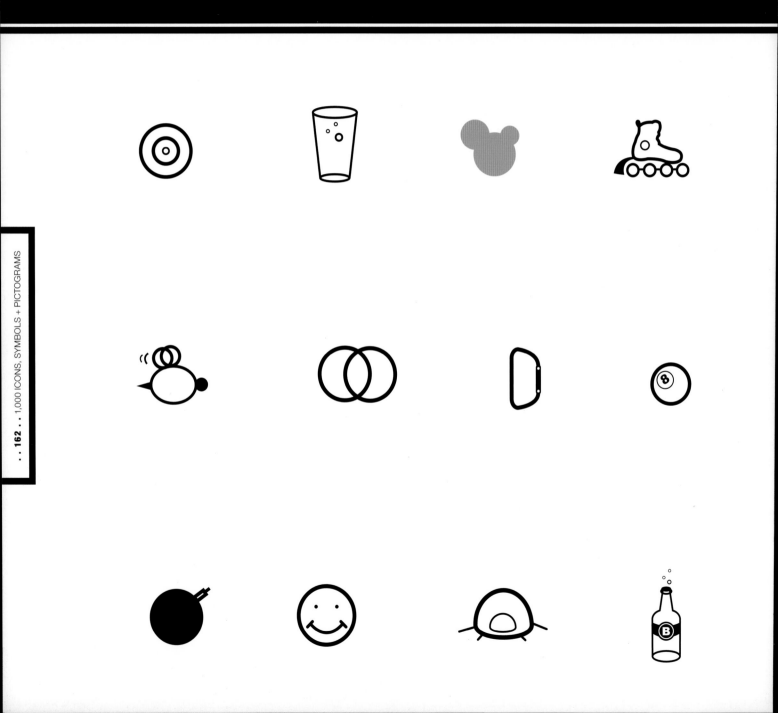

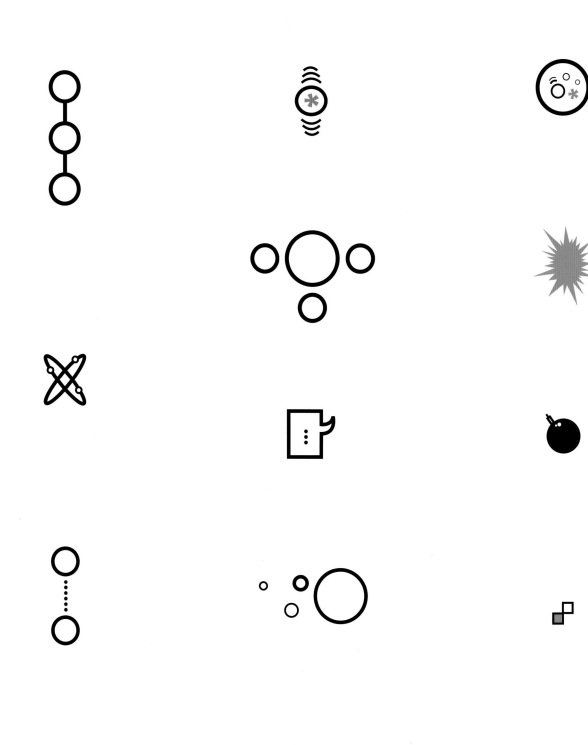

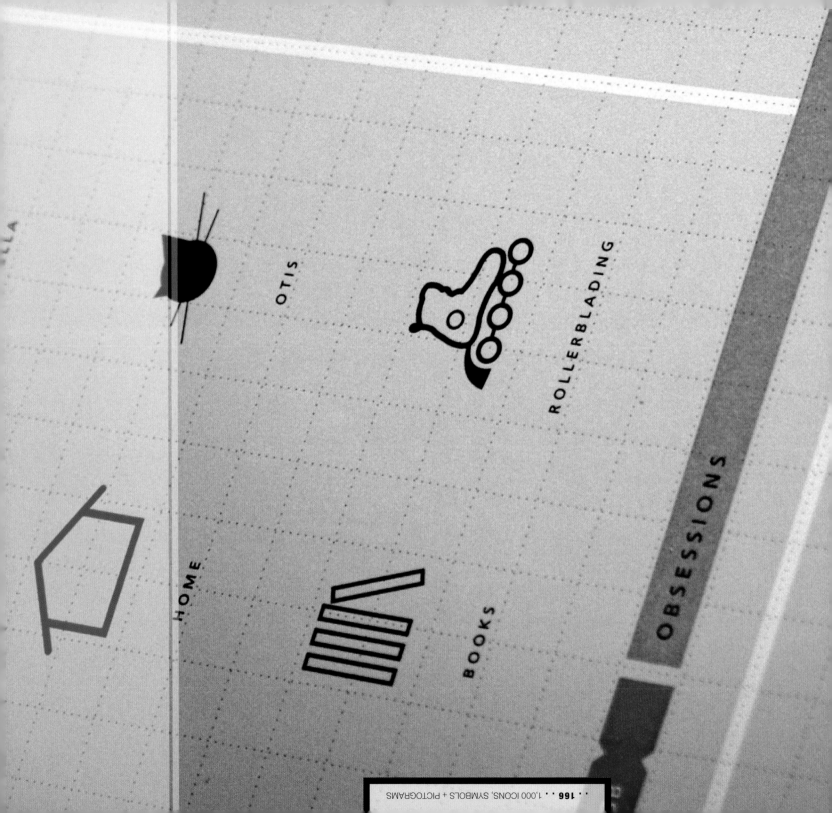

OTIS

ROLLERBLADING

OBSESSIONS

HOME

BOOKS

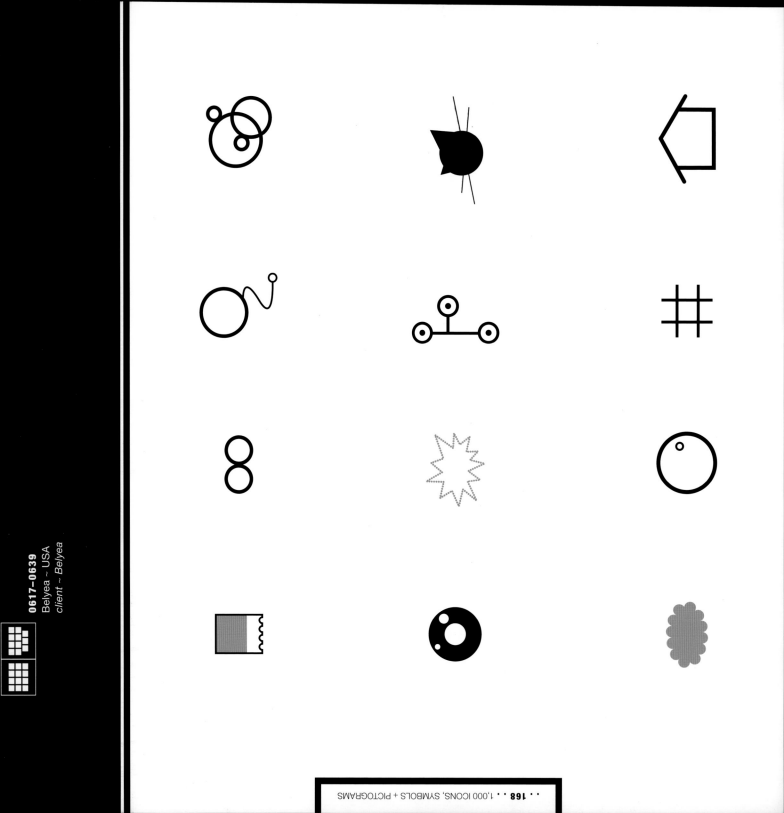

0617-0639
Belyea ~ USA
client ~ Belyea

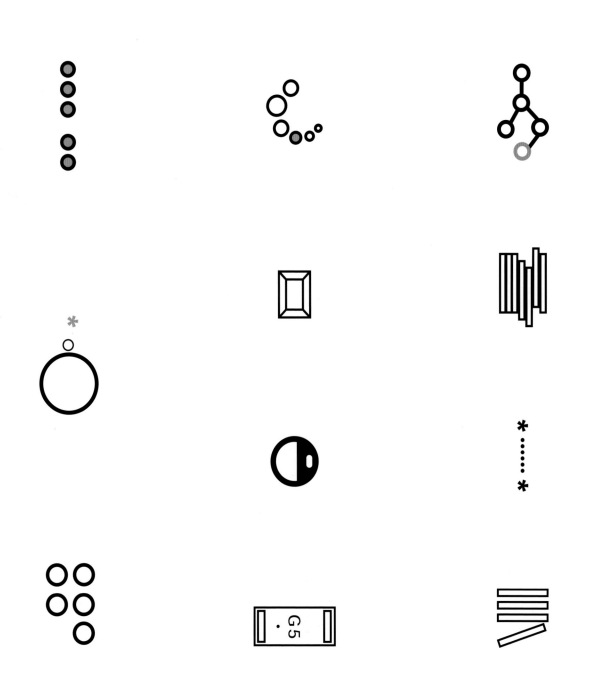

0640-0641

subcommunication ~ Canada
client ~ Chambly Martin Newspaper

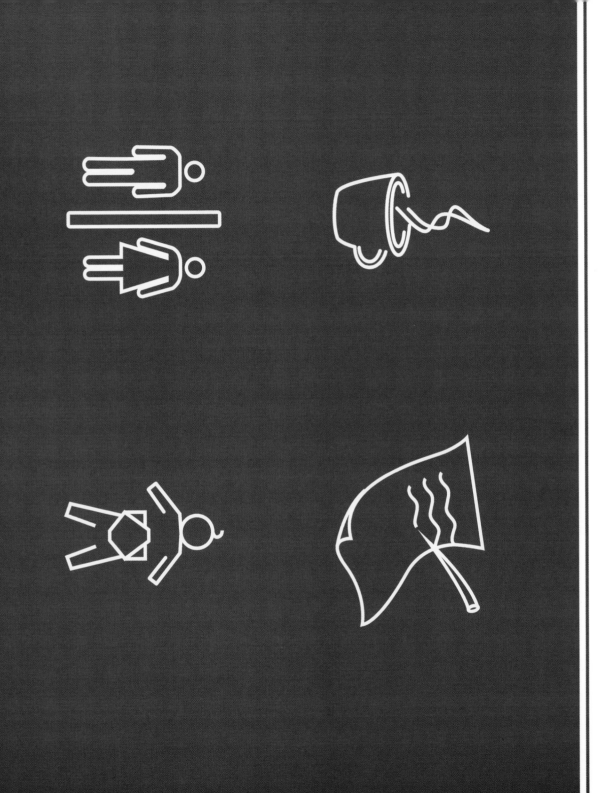

0644-0647

sky design ~ USA

client ~ Forum

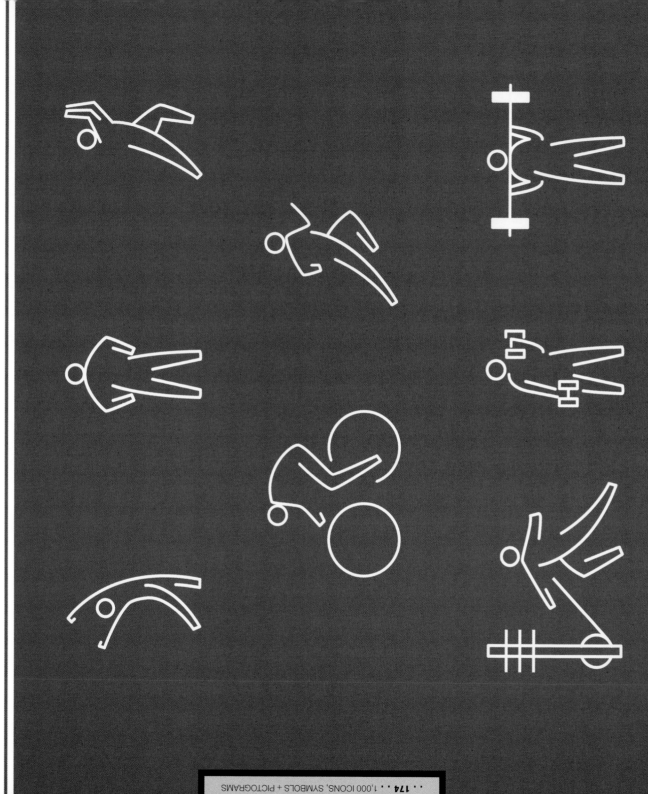

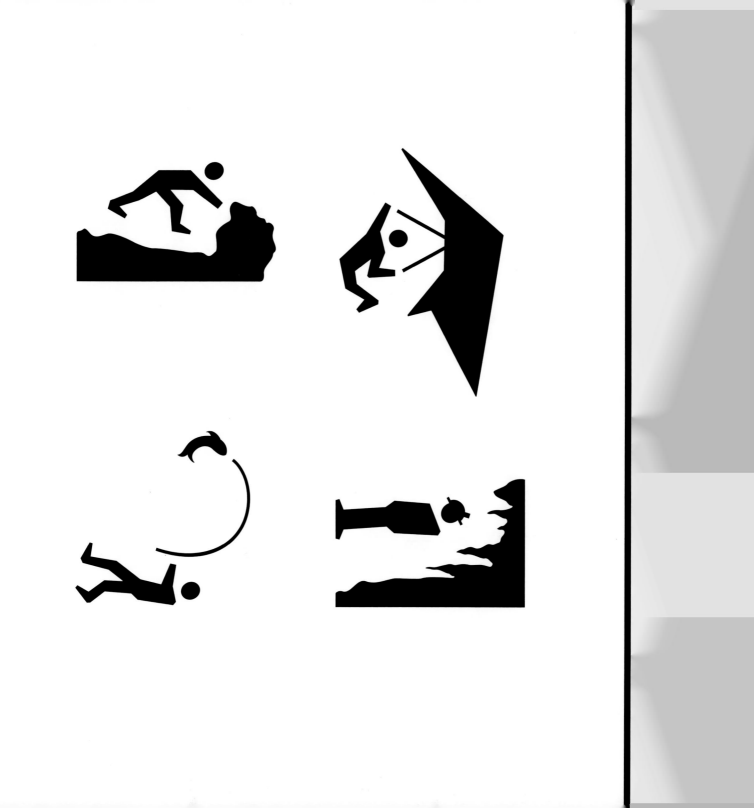

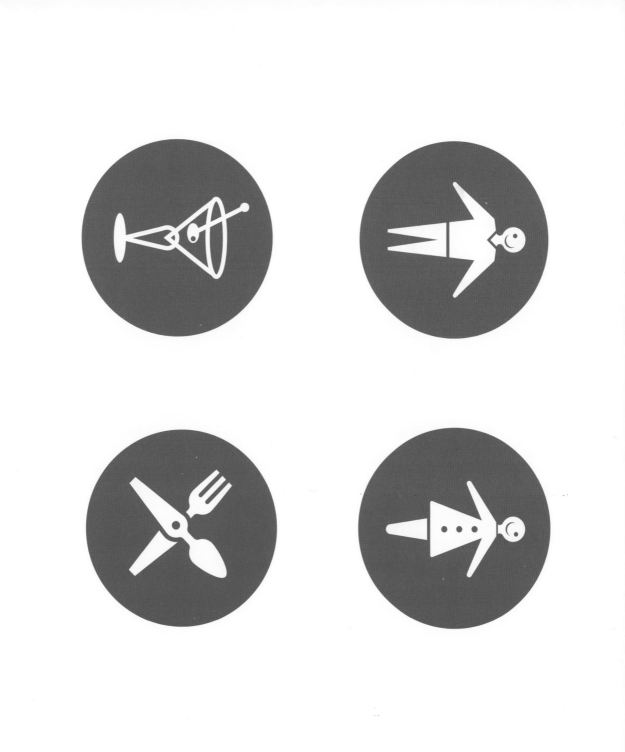

0672–0675
Sayles Graphic Design ~ USA
client ~ American Institute of Architects

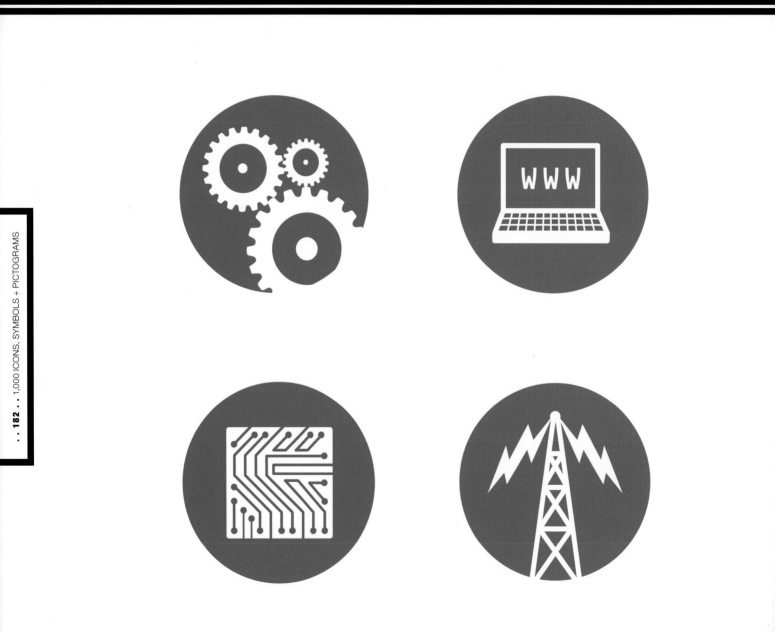

0676-0678
TnTom Design ~ USA
client ~ Atomic-Fusion for sologig.com

RACING

SIGHTS

DINING AND
ENTERTAINMENT

0679–0683
Sayles Graphic Design ~ USA
client ~ Knoxville Chamber of Commerce

0684–0695
mgmt.design ~ USA
client ~ The New York Times

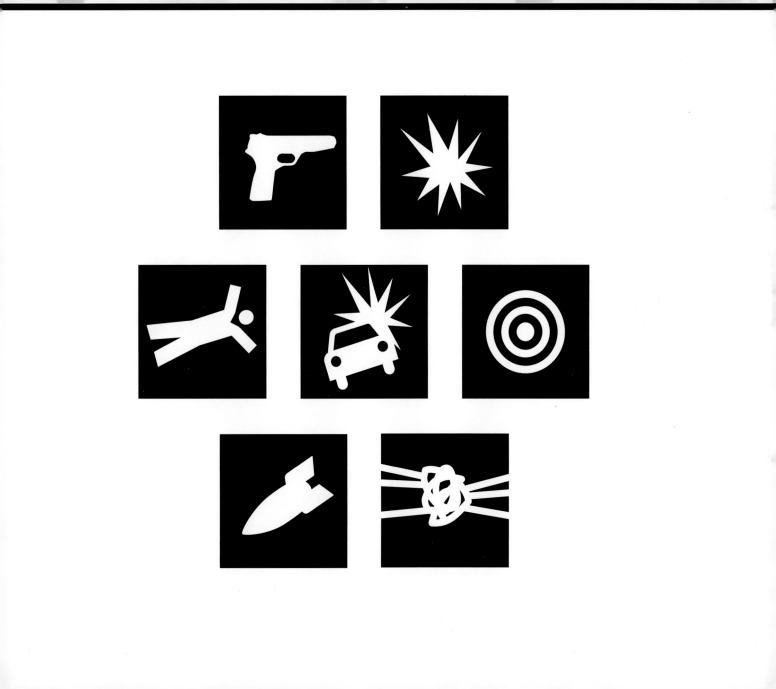

Op-Chart

ADRIANA LINS de ALBUQUERQUE AND ALICIA CHENG

14 Days in Iraq

eeks of January, at least 202 people died as a result of the in-
e killings have been indiscriminate. The dead include Iraqi offi-
s, civilians and, of course, Iraqi, American and coalition soldiers.
wn here took place across the country, but there is a clear concentra-
alled Sunni Triangle, which stretches from Tikrit in the north to Bagh-
st and to Falluja and Ramadi in the west.
the daily toll is noted by the news media in headlines and video clips,

many Americans have a hard time incorporating these individual pieces of information into a coherent image over time. The map below, based on Pentagon data and
news reports, shows the number killed and wounded since Jan. 1. Because of the lim-
its placed on reporters and the military's need to inform families, there may have
been additional casualties during this period that are not noted here. The map also
does not include Iraqi civilians accidentally killed by coalition forces. Still, it is an
attempt to visually depict the human cost of a foreign in an embattled land.

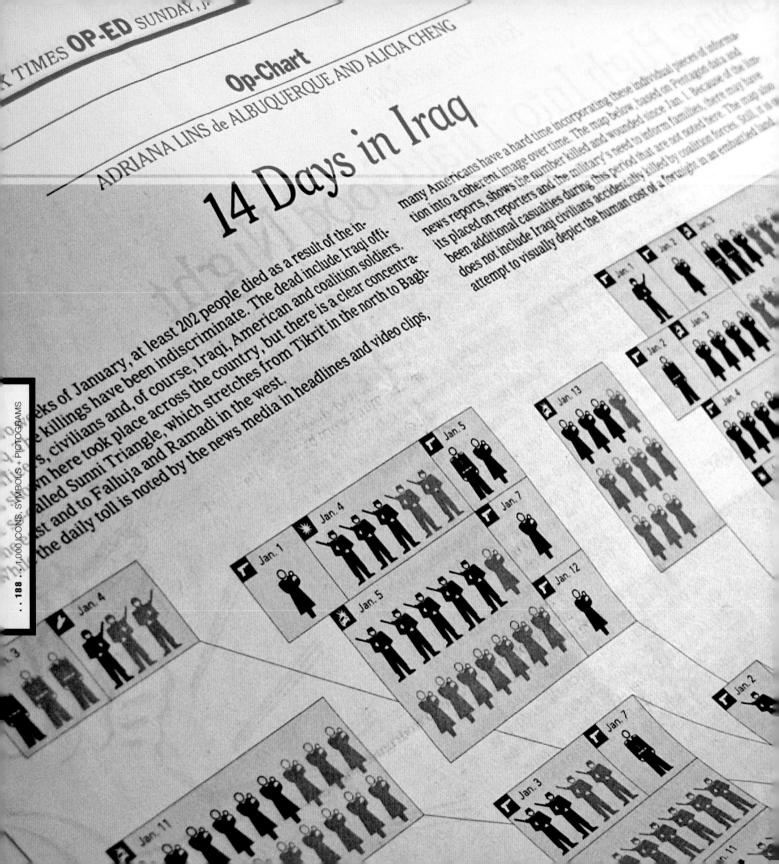

0696—0701
Dresser Johnson ~ USA
client ~ Two Twelve Associates/Radio City Music Hall

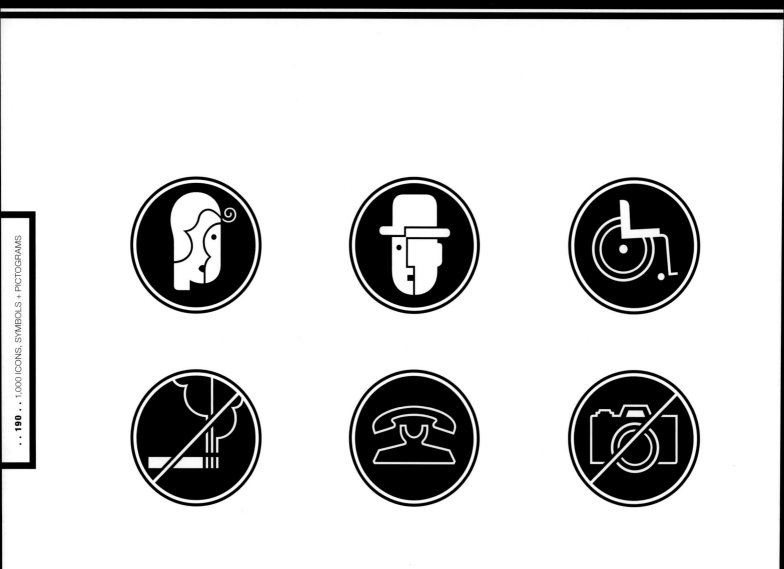

LADIES' LOUNGE

WHEELCHAIR ACCESSIBLE
RESTROOMS ARE LOCATED
IN THE GRAND LOUNGE

Blackcoffee ~ USA
client ~ The Rockport Company

USA

WORLD SHOE ASSO

ROCKPORT E

SANDS EXP

FEBR

0702–0704
Blackcoffee ~ USA
client ~ The Rockport Company

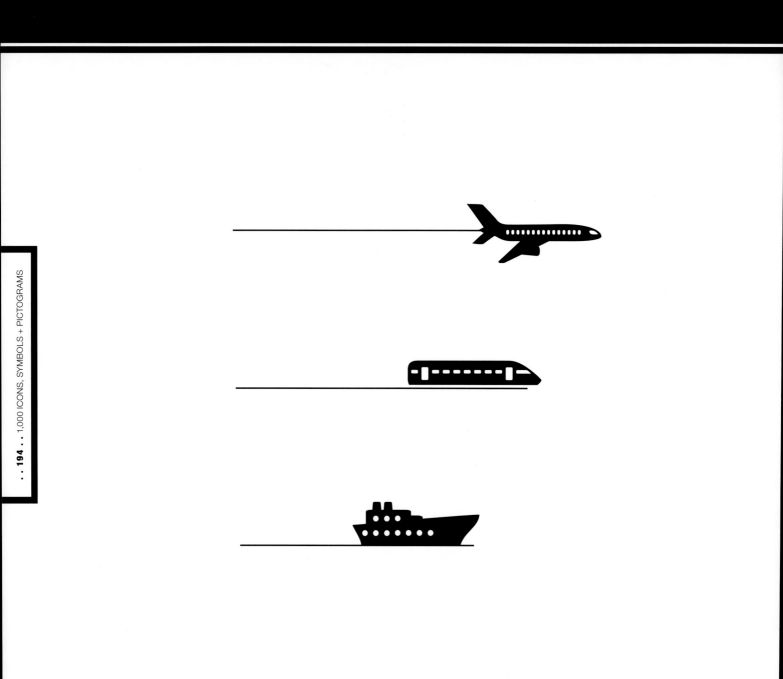

0705
Blackcoffee ~ USA
client ~ Gary Tardiff Studio

0706–0707
Blackcoffee ~ USA
client ~ Blackcoffee

Bash

join Blackoffee

extraordinaire .

ne on down .

t on the town .

to see you there .

BLACKCOFFEE

Blackcoffee ~ USA
client ~ Blackcoffee

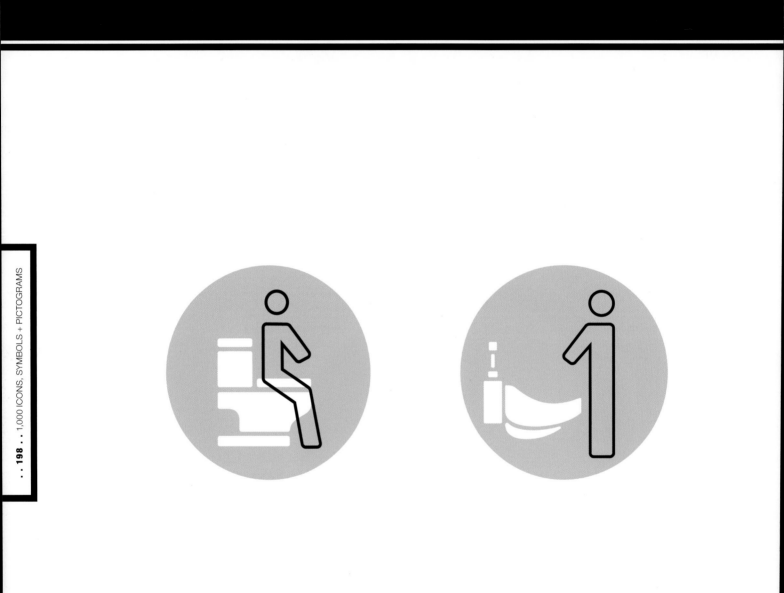

0710–0713
Gardner Design ~ USA
client ~ Gardner Design

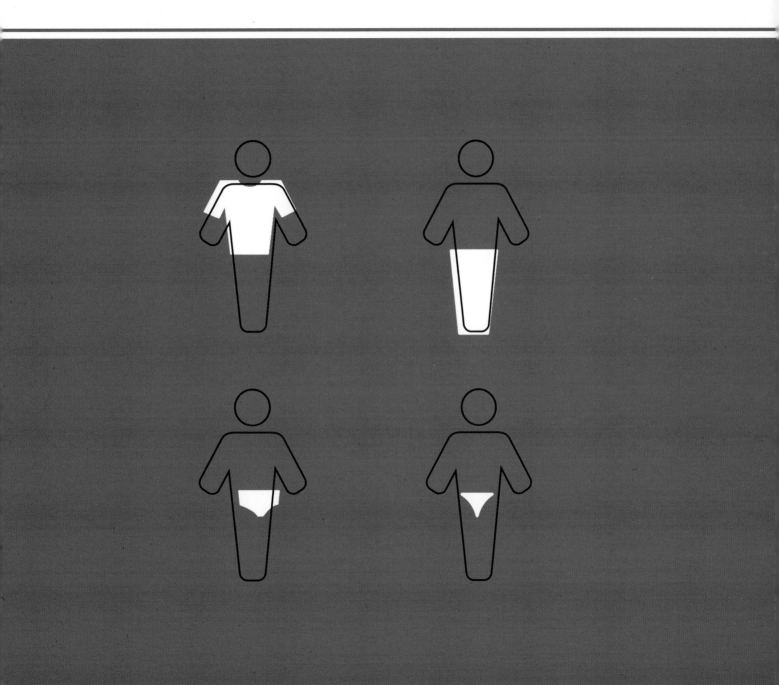

0714-0716
UNIT-Y ~ USA
client ~ Sony Electronics

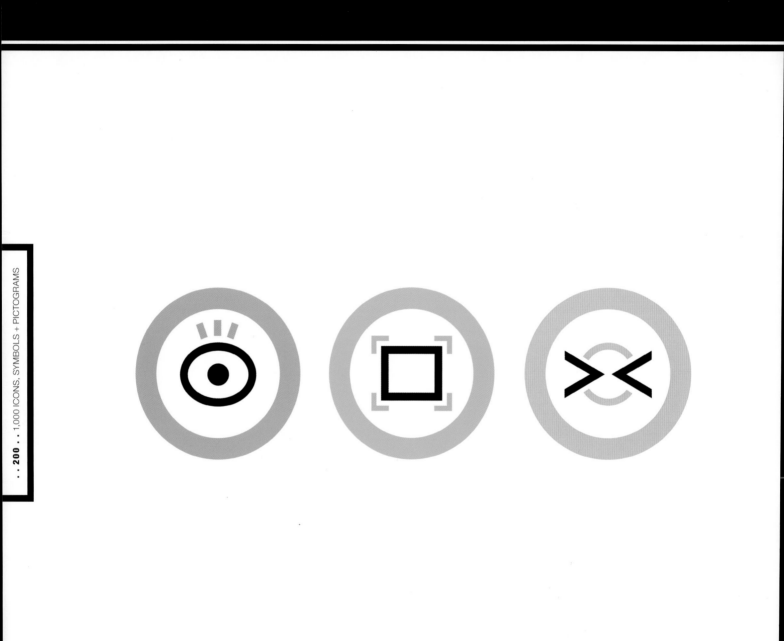

Mirko Ilić Corp. ~ USA
client ~ *Publikum*

$E=mc^2$

То инат пркоста
да прписују себи. Покоји
да је на високој цени.
рачуни тот ината, планета
животиња, по правил
високи. У нешто бенит
јанти везује се за спе
„Из ината“ српски
тимови су
способни да
победе
и

ривојива од
СЛЕТА.
изажене
малу Титу,
ма кроз
ају.

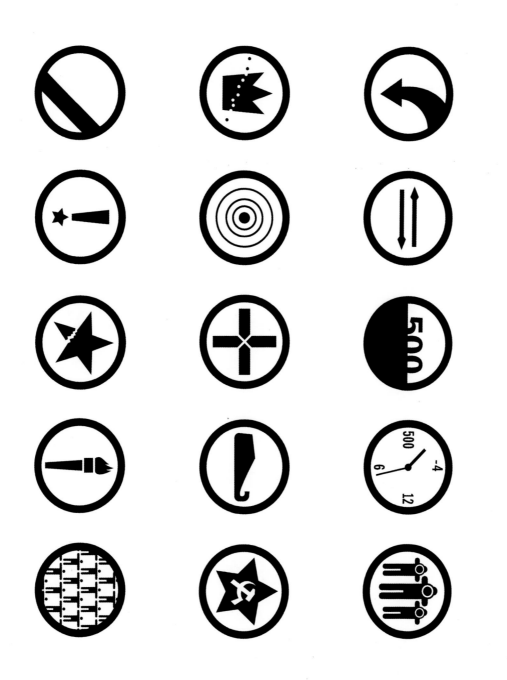

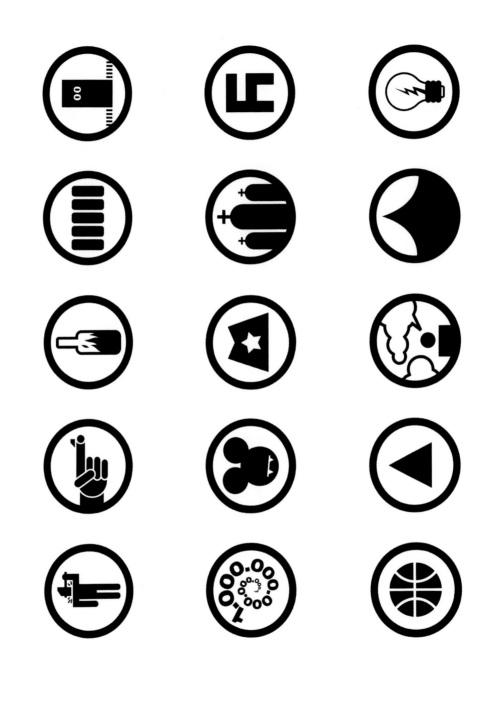

17

Mirko Ilić Corp. ~ USA
client ~ Publikum

E=mc³

31

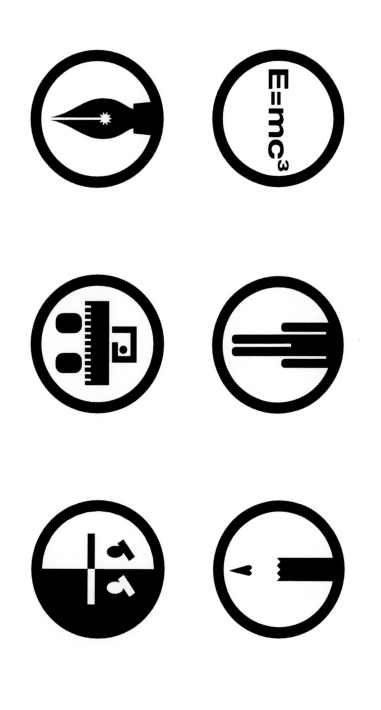

$E=mc^3$

0751–0756
Mirko Ilić Corp. ~ USA
client ~ Publikum

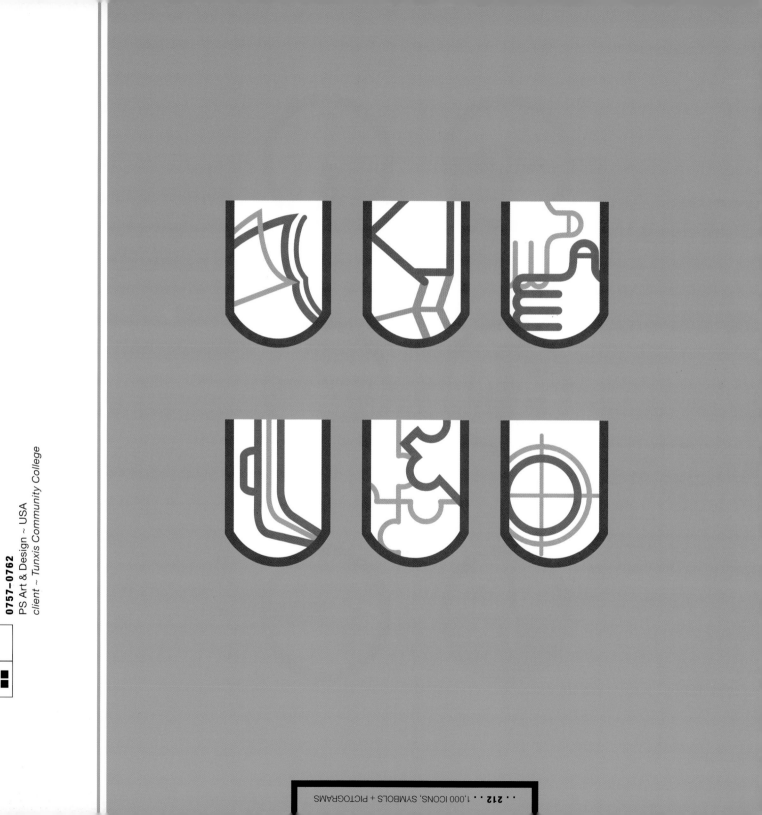

0763–0766
Rickabaugh Graphics ~ USA
client ~ Luckie & Co./Alabama

0767–0771

sky design ~ USA
client ~ Fry Reglet

sky design ~ USA
client ~ Fry Reglet

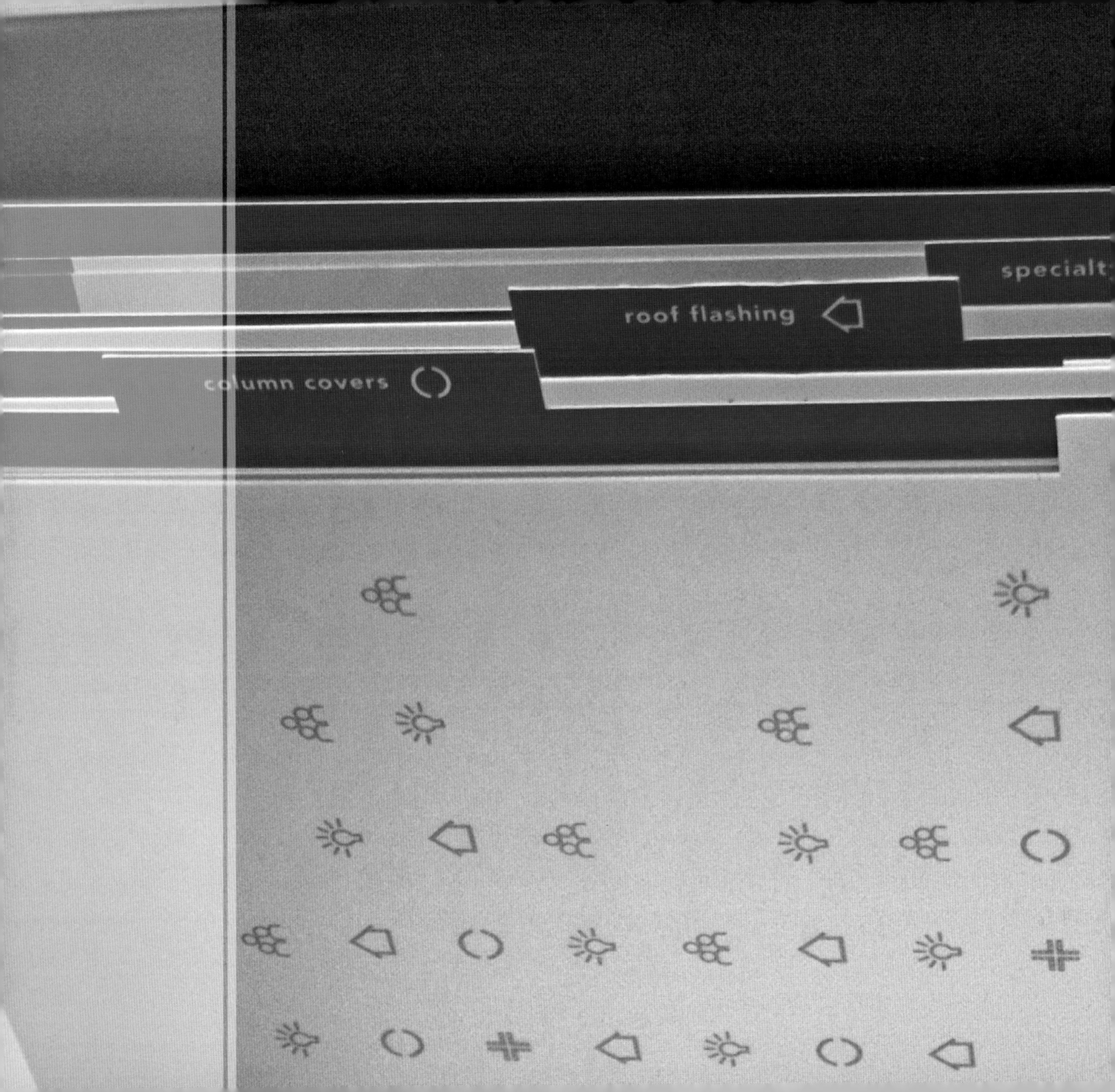

column covers ()

roof flashing ▷

specialty

0772-0775

Stoltze Design ~ USA
client ~ Profit Logic

PLACE

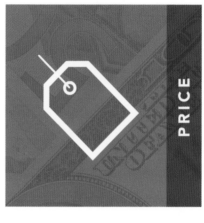

PRICE

PLAN

PROMOTE

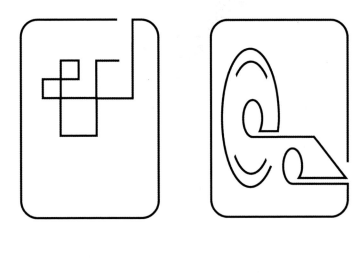
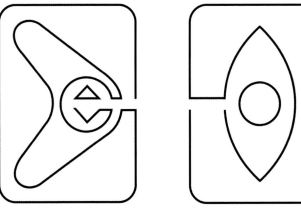

0780–0781

Wallace Church, Inc. ~ USA
client ~ Wallace Church, Inc.

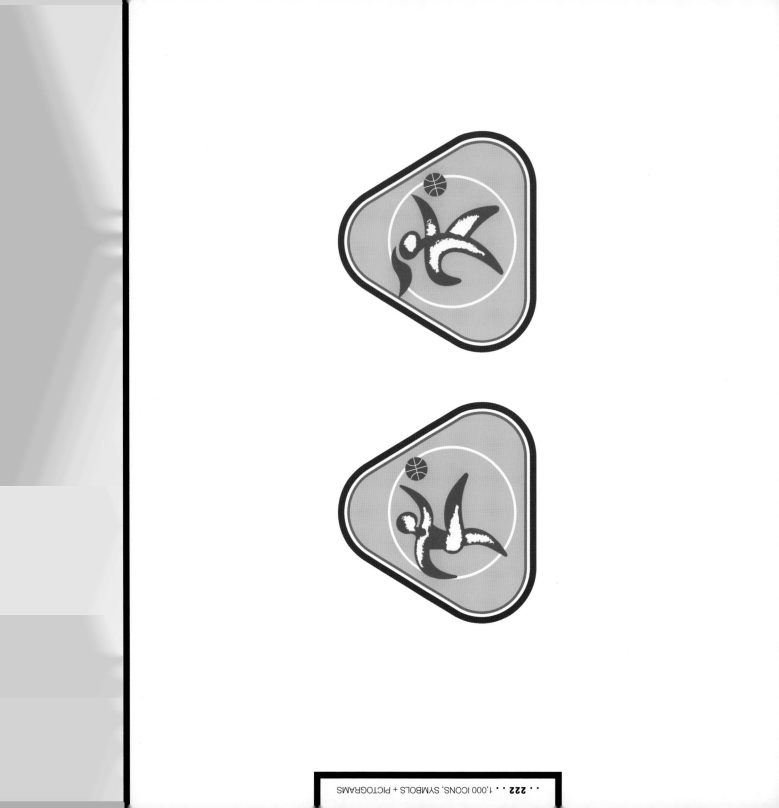

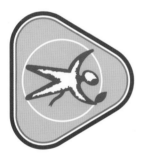

Sayles Graphic Design ~ USA
client ~ Amateur Athletic Union

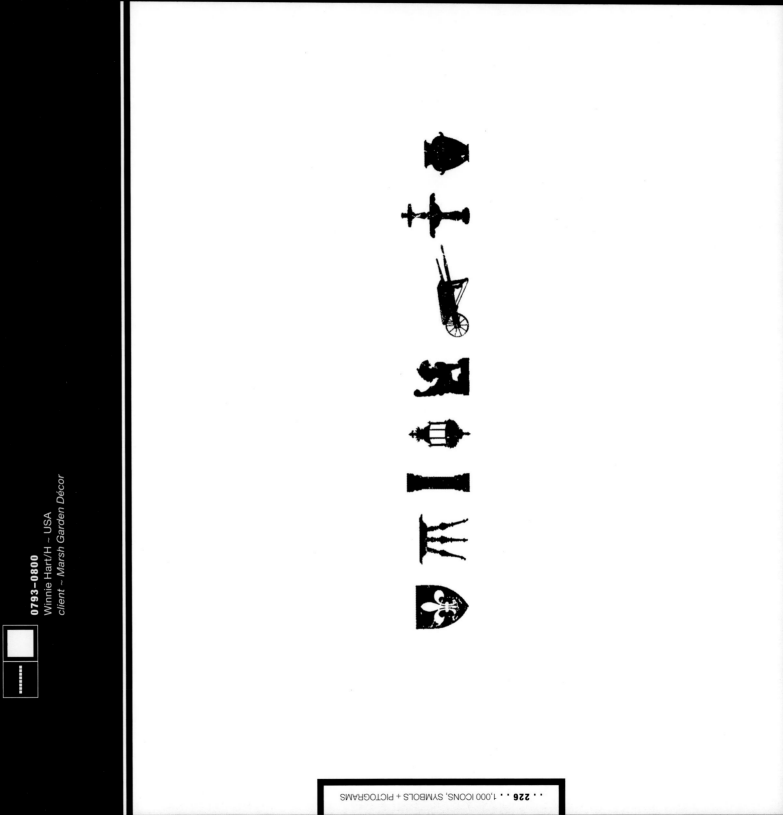

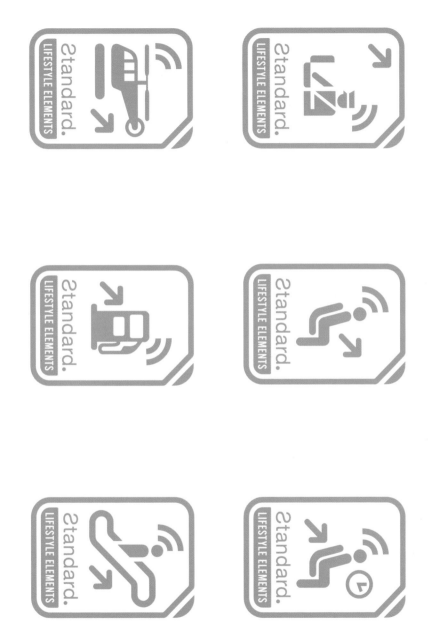

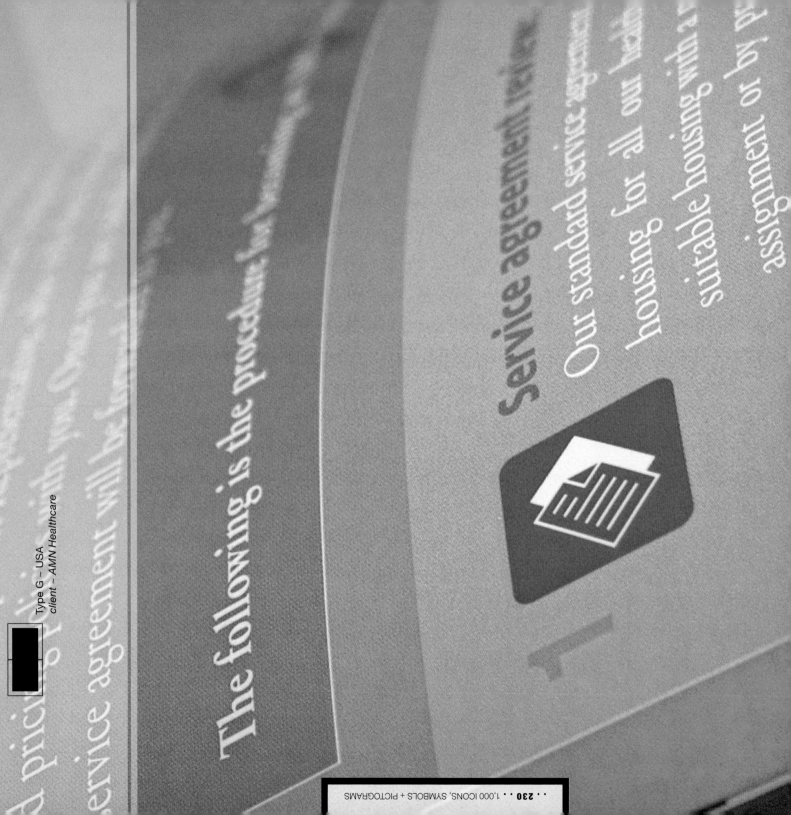

0810-0821
Type G ~ USA
client ~ AMN Healthcare

0822–0824

LSD ~ Spain

client ~ Juan Carlos Ibáñes & Gema Díaz

Nos complace invitaros a nuestra boda a las 1
que celebraremos el 23 de marzo Virgen Gra
en la Iglesia de la Virgen de la —Torrela
Plaza Baldomero Iglesias Iglesias—Torrela

0825–0827

LSD ~ Spain

client ~ Juan Carlos Ibáñes & Gema Díaz

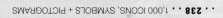

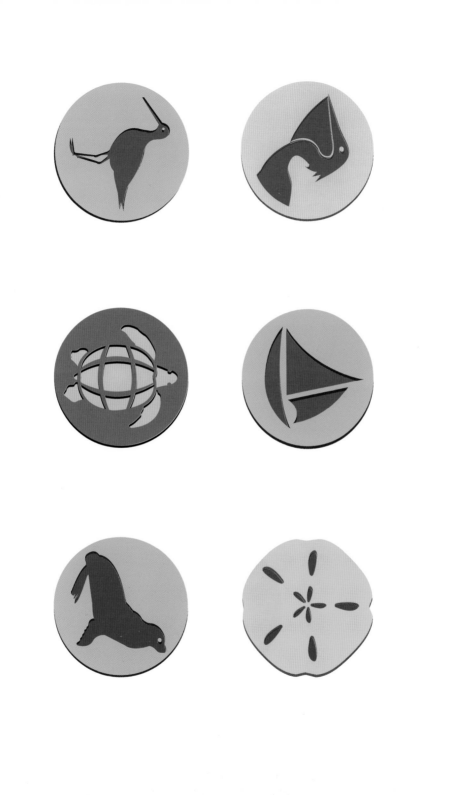

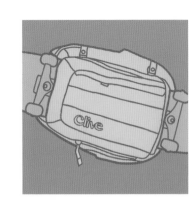

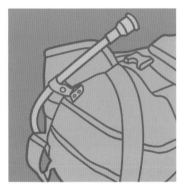

Type G ~ USA
client ~ Clive Backpacks

Clive

FALL 03

Board Carrier System (BCS)

It's you and your board from point A... it 8 as one stable unit. Boards carried vertically and/or... depending on the pack.

No Spill Gusset (NSG)

A simple solution to a big problem. Gussets prevent content loss while still allowing easy accessibility to main and side compartments.

Pro Pocket (PRO)

The name says it all. Clive supports a dedicated team of athletes who abuse their gear as much as they use it. Pro Packs are an extension of the athletes' lifestyles; personalizes the athletes' personalities and vision.

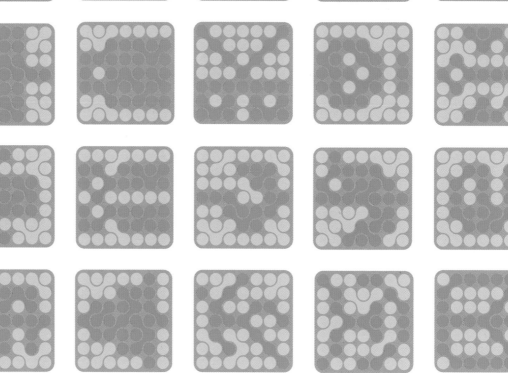

0872–0878

Stoltze Design ~ USA

client ~ Massachusetts College of Art

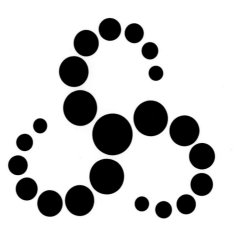

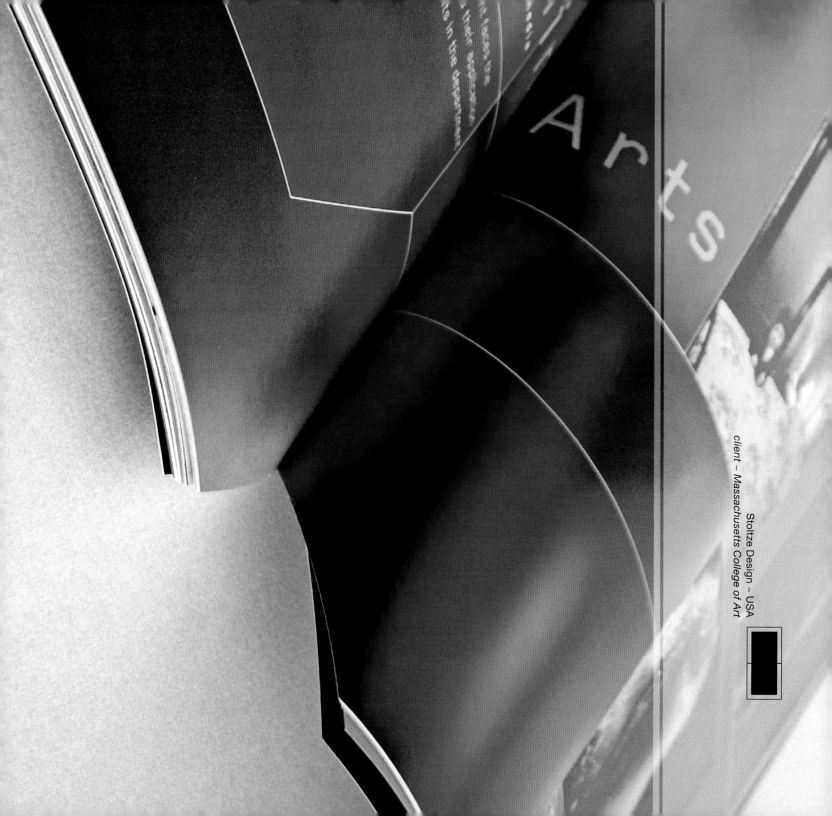

Arts

Stoltze Design ~ USA
client ~ Massachusetts College of Art

0879–0884

sky design ~ USA
client ~ EarthLink

ELECTRICAL

ELECTRICAL

MEN

MEN

MECHANICAL

MECHANICAL

WOMEN

WOMEN

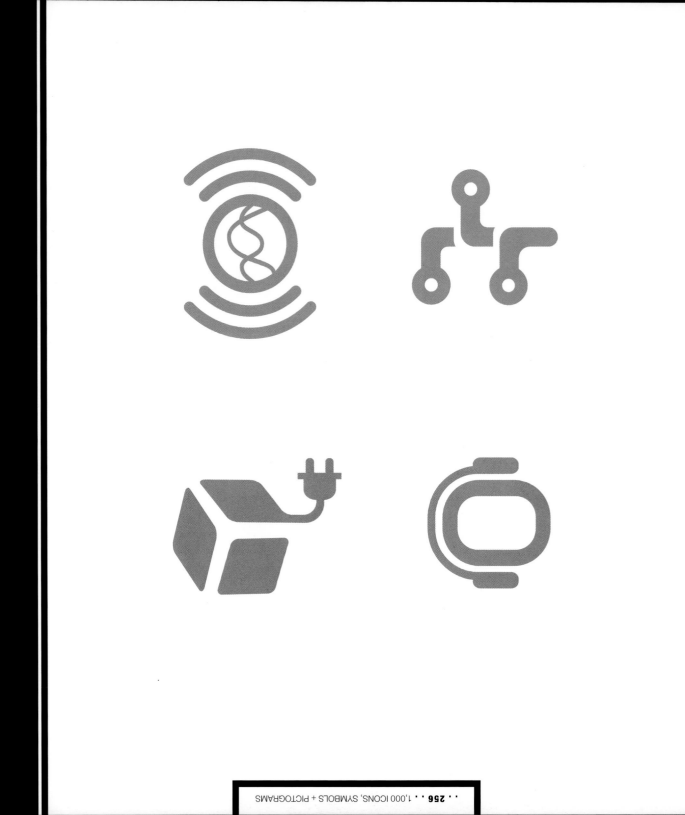

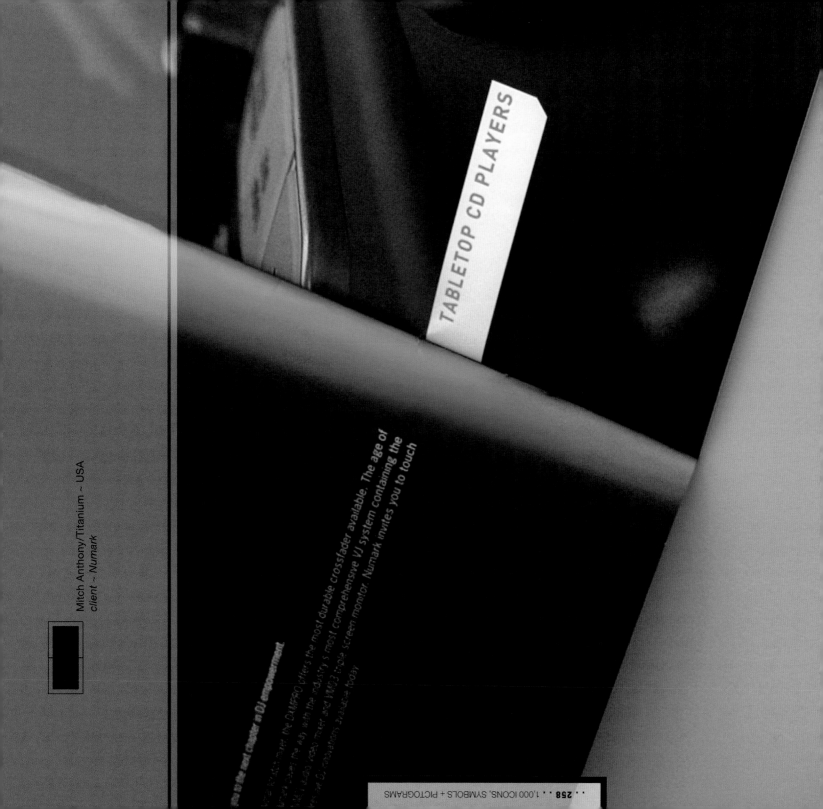

TABLETOP CD PLAYERS

Mitch Anthony/Titanium ~ USA
client ~ Numark

...to the end closer in DJ empowerment.

...to support the DAVPRO offers the most durable crossfader available. The age of ... the A51 with the industry's most comprehensive VJ system containing the ... Audio video mixer and VM03 triple screen monitor. Numark invites you to touch ... corresponding available today.

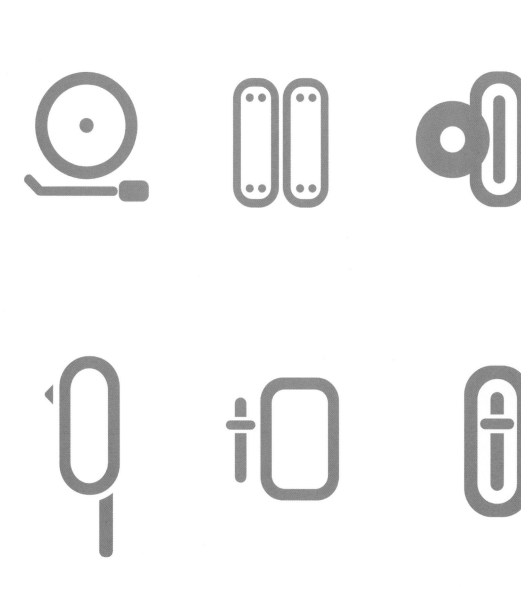

0889-0894

Mitch Anthony/Titanium ~ USA

client ~ Numark

0895-0905
Joe Miller's Company ~ USA
client ~ Hewlett-Packard

0906-0918

Joe Miller's Company ~ USA
client ~ Hewlett-Packard

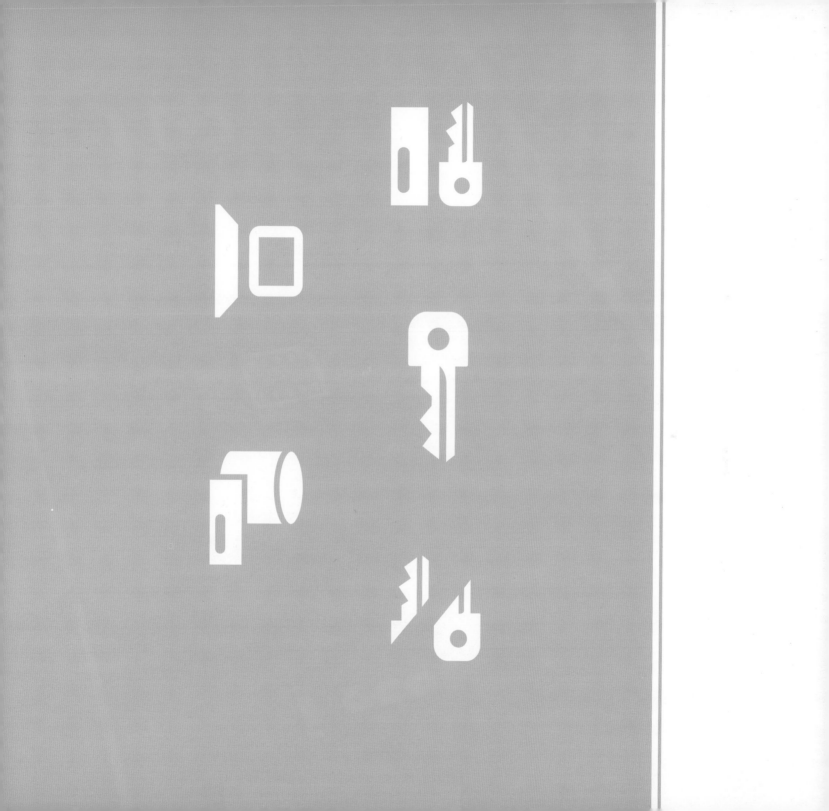

VIDEO

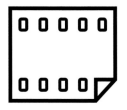

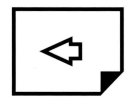

As soluções integradas por ramo da telefonia incluem o seguinte:

ARBOR®/WIRELINE

Como provedor de serviços de telefonia fixa, seja de transmissão de voz ou serviços de dados, sua empresa enfrenta um ambiente competitivo e complexo. Desregulamentação, novas tecnologias, e novos competidores têm contribuído para o contexto atual - um mundo de novas oportunidades tanto para os provedores já estabelecidos como para os que entram agora no mercado. Tirar proveito dessas oportunidades involve desafios consideráveis. Para ser competitiva, sua empresa deve implementar ofertas diferenciadas e promover respostas rápidas e afinadas com os requisitos de seu mercado consumidor.

Arbor/Wireline é uma solução ampla que atende tanto operadoras novas como as de reputação estabelecida no mercado. Como provedor de serviços de voz e dados, você pode se beneficiar da capacidade de serviços de tarifação avançada oferecida pelo Arbor/Wireline que inclui recursos como tarifação agregada, corredor, tarifas jurisdicionais, tarifa de amplo circuito, assim como o suporte a varejo e grandes clientes incluindo revenda de serviços. ... disponíveis no Arbor/Wireline para a administração integrada ... atribuição de números de telefone individuais ou em ...torizadas, ou por regiões.

Customer Su

CEGET
ELEC

INTERNET

BROADBAND

MOBILE

WIRELINE

BROADBAND

MOBILE

WIRELINE

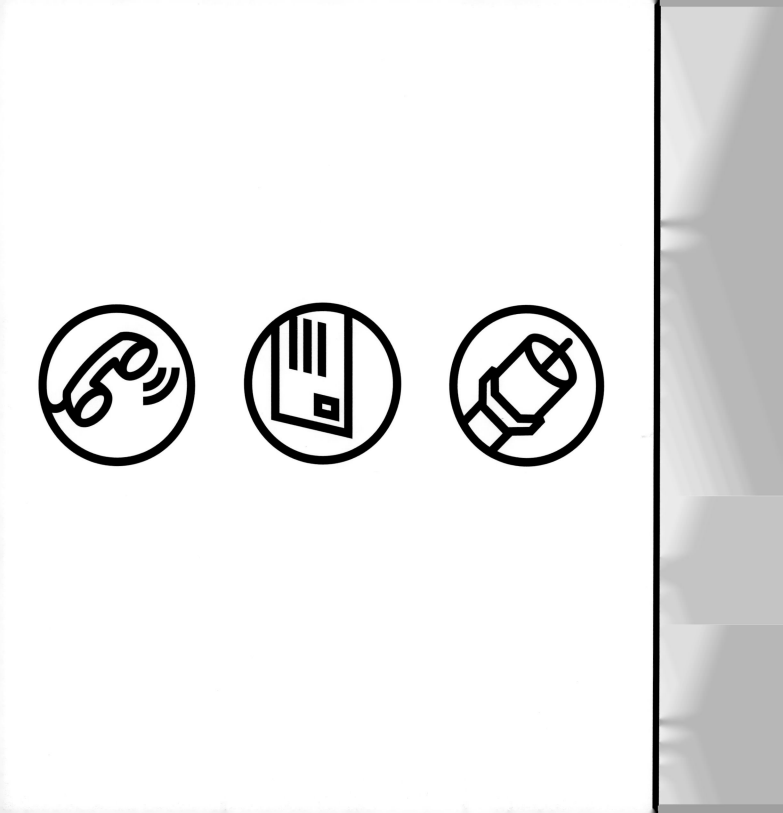

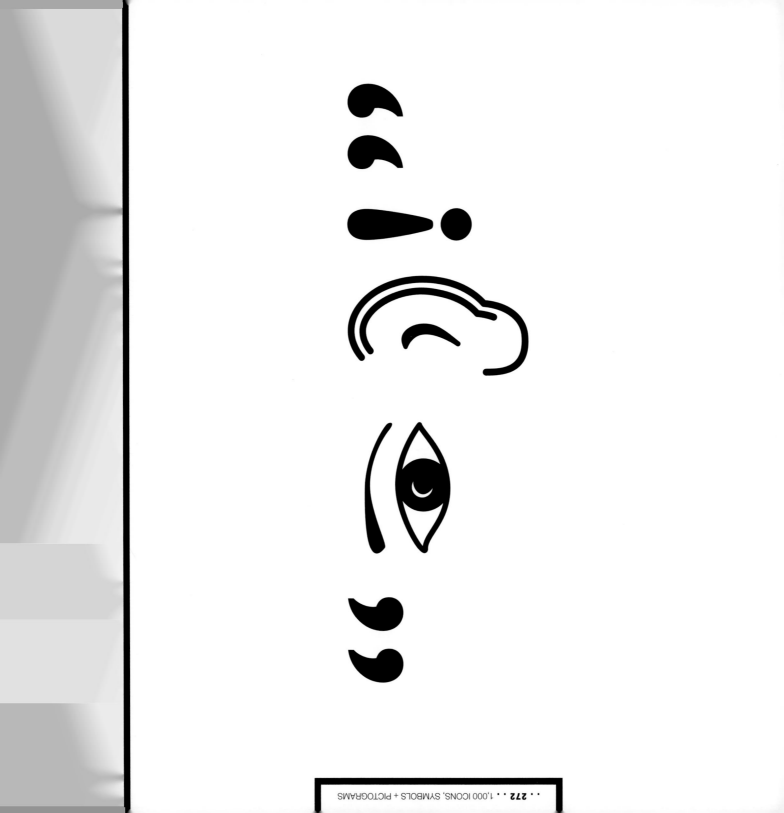

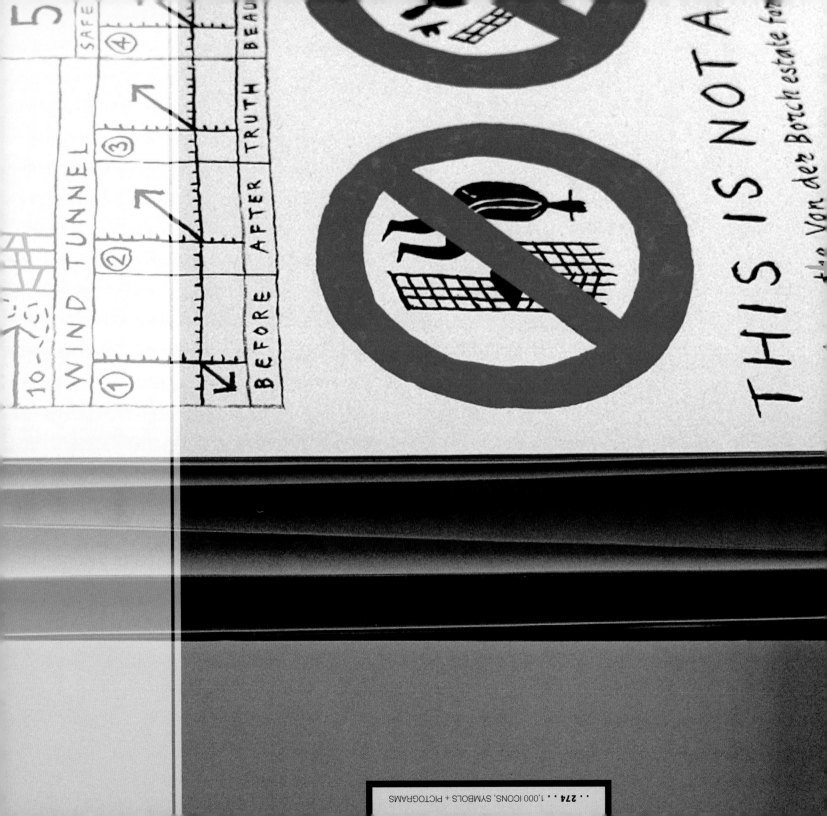

THIS IS NOT A

the Von der Borch estate for

5				SAFE ④
	WIND TUNNEL			
10-'5"	①	②	③	
	BEFORE	AFTER	TRUTH	BEAU

2. Usually a holder for the IC is attache...
If necessary the conn... parts have
be bent a bit (with a small pair of plier...
For this purpose a narrow side of the...

value of resistor before fitting.

is marked; with a notch, a point impre...
a deepened triangle or something like that. In...
rare cases the vertical is not marked at...

3. These products do not have any CE accepta...
May contain substances which are harmfu...
to the body. Dangerous situations may o...
during starting when making a mistake (e...
cables may glow or catch fire) The prese...
of a competant person is always necessa...
during mounting. If the module or devic...
does not work properly, accidents happe...
(liquid ran into the device, device fell dow...
etc.) or if it causes strange noises or...
smells, switch off immediately. Ask an...
expert for examination.

4. BORCH/FISHER disclaim any responsib...
for anything they have done in the past o...
anything they might do in the fut...

HAPPY HOLI...
FROM

Let them have me
to myself. I look...
me stepped into...

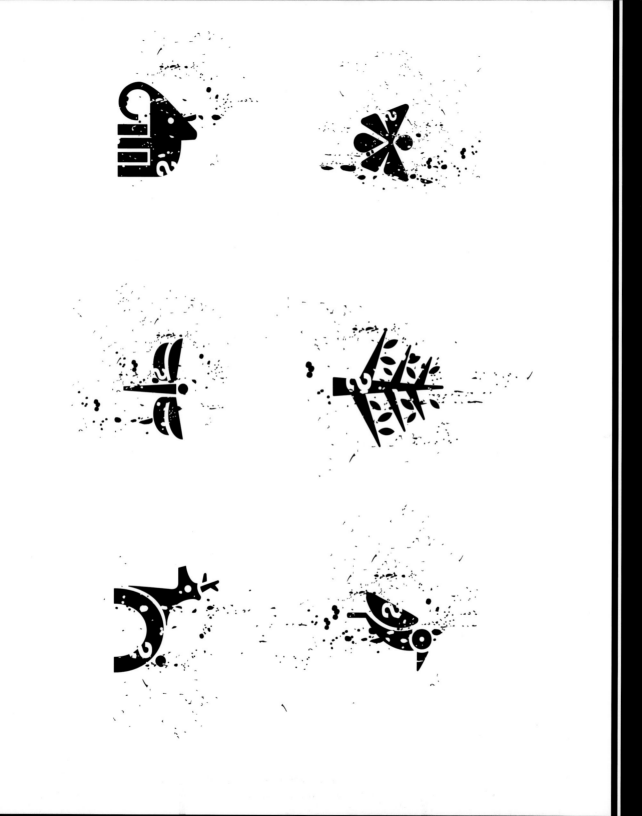

0932–0937

Gardner Design ~ USA

client ~ Standard

0938–0940
Ideentity ~ Germany
client ~ systemtrans e.k.

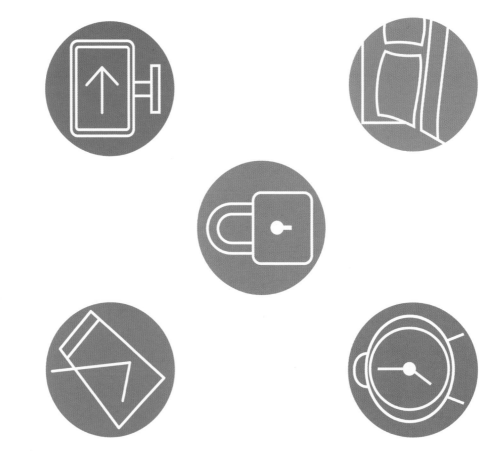

0941–0950

Atlas Communications ~ USA
client ~ Atomic Kitchen Design

The Top My Rooms

Safety & Security

Wake-up C

Atlas Communiciations ~ USA
client ~ Atomic Kitchen Design

0951–0960

Atlas Communications ~ USA

client ~ Atomic Kitchen Design

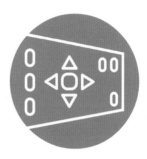

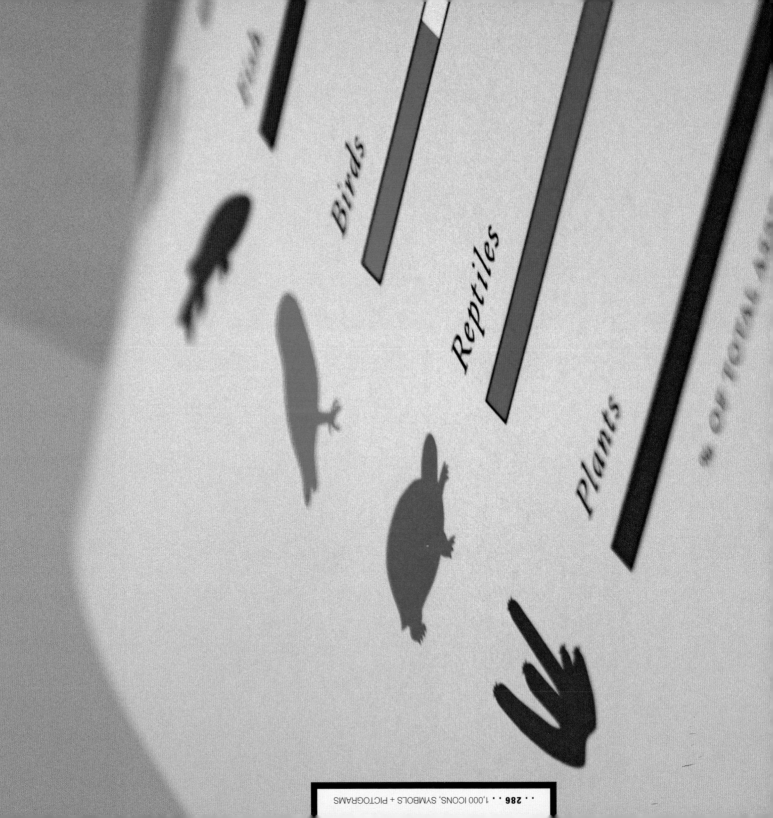

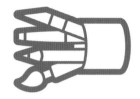

0972-0974

Glitschka Studios ~ USA

client ~ www.creativelatitude.com

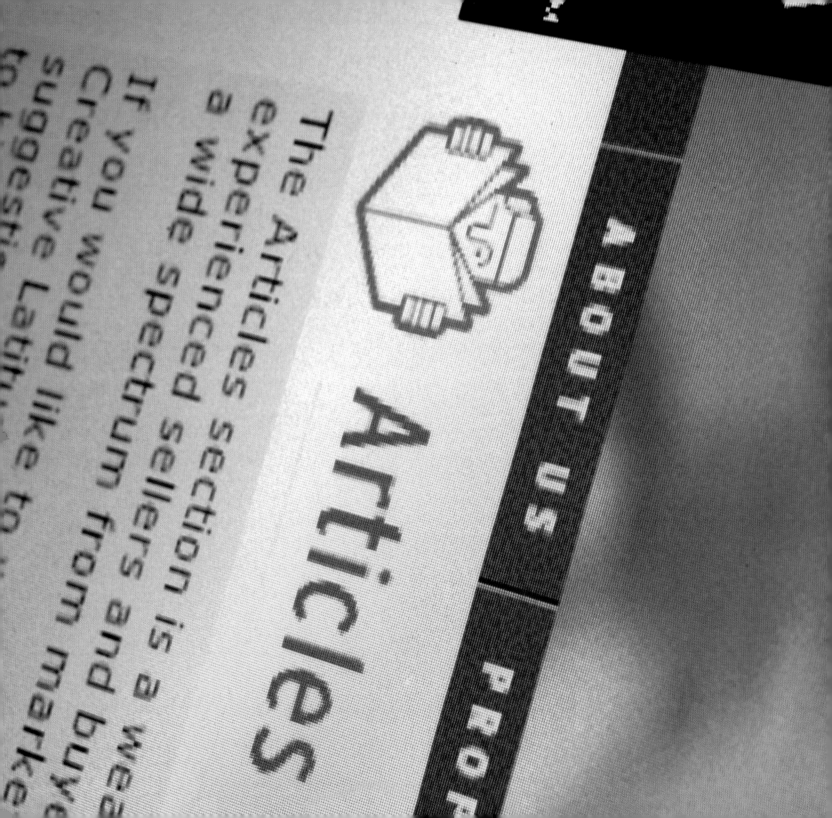

Articles

The Articles experienced section is a wide spectrum of Creative sellers and buyers. If you would like to suggest Latit...

0975-0986

Glitschka Studios ~ USA

client ~ www.creativelatitude.com

0987–0991

Ideas Frescas ~ UK
client ~ MA Communication Design/Central Martins College
of Art & Design and the Embassy of El Salvador in London

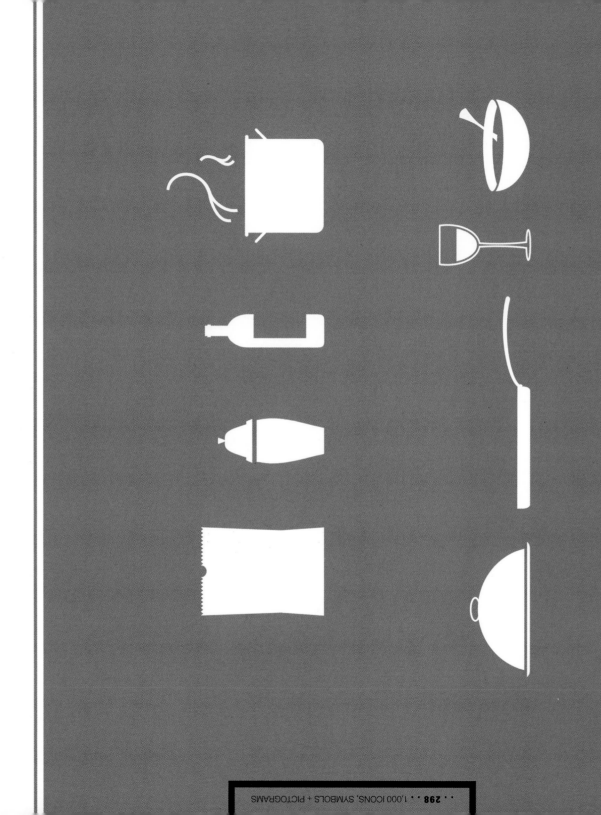

0992-1000

Blackcoffee ~ USA
client ~ Gary Tardiff Studio

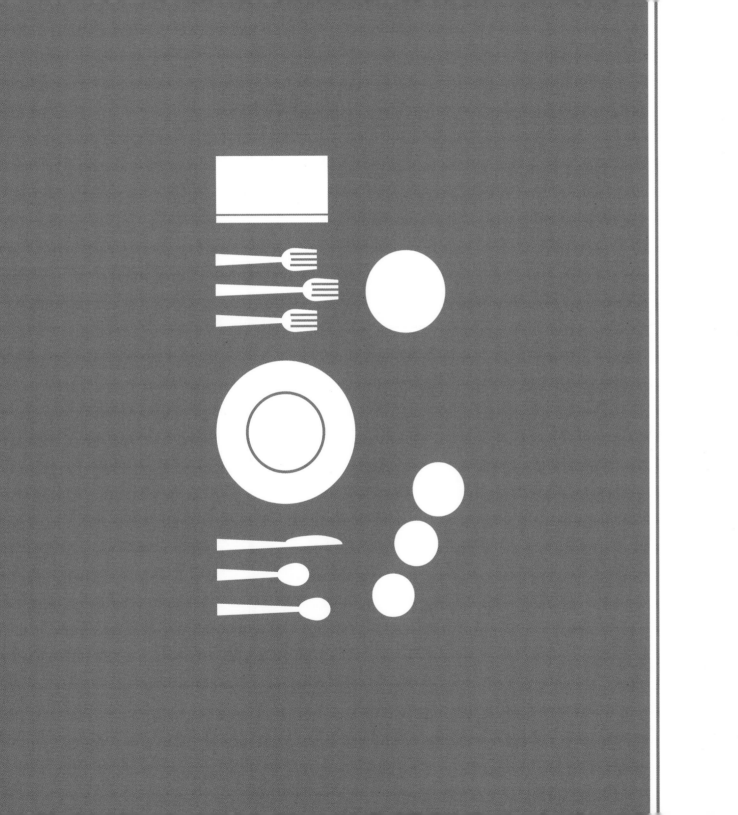

contents: galleries

1000

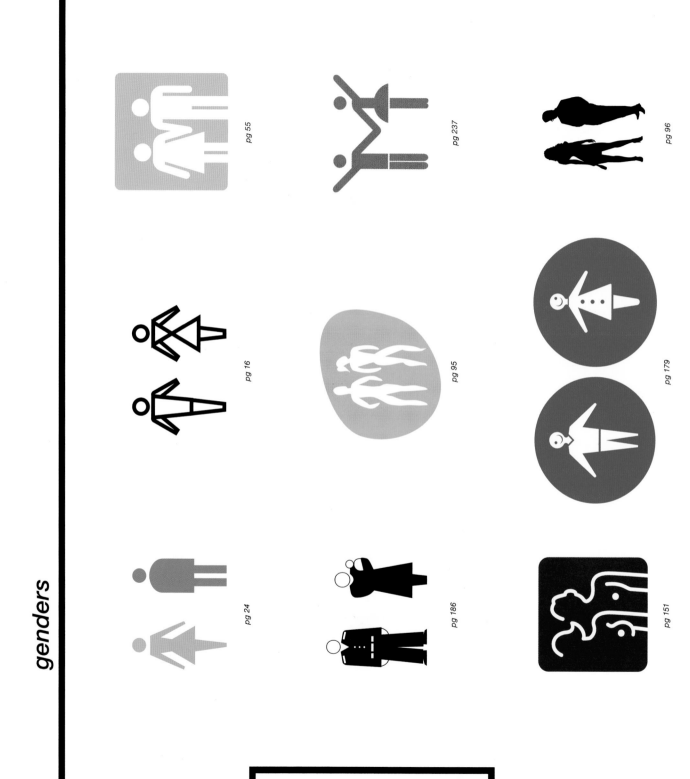

genders

pg 55

pg 237

pg 96

pg 16

pg 95

pg 179

pg 24

pg 186

pg 151

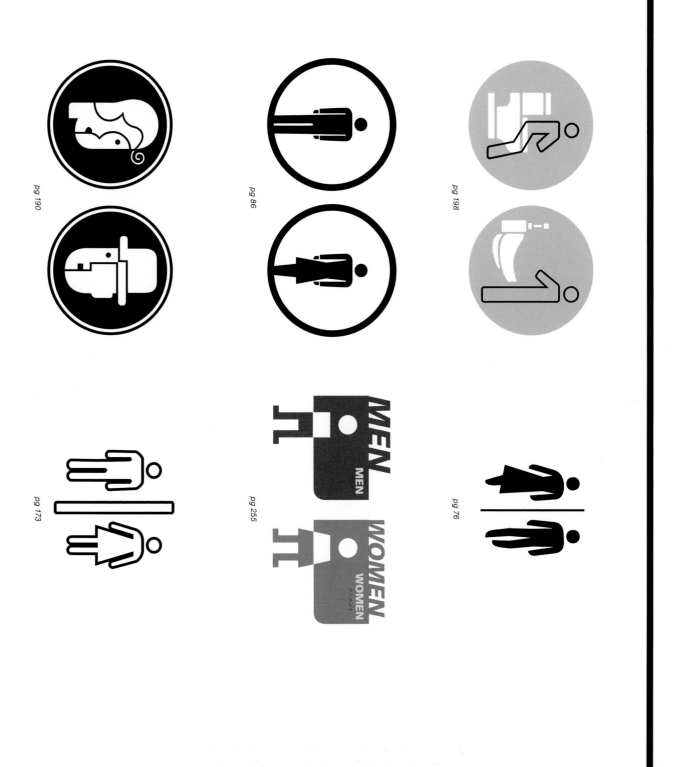

pg 190
pg 86
pg 198
pg 173
pg 255
pg 76

MEN

MEN

WOMEN

WOMEN

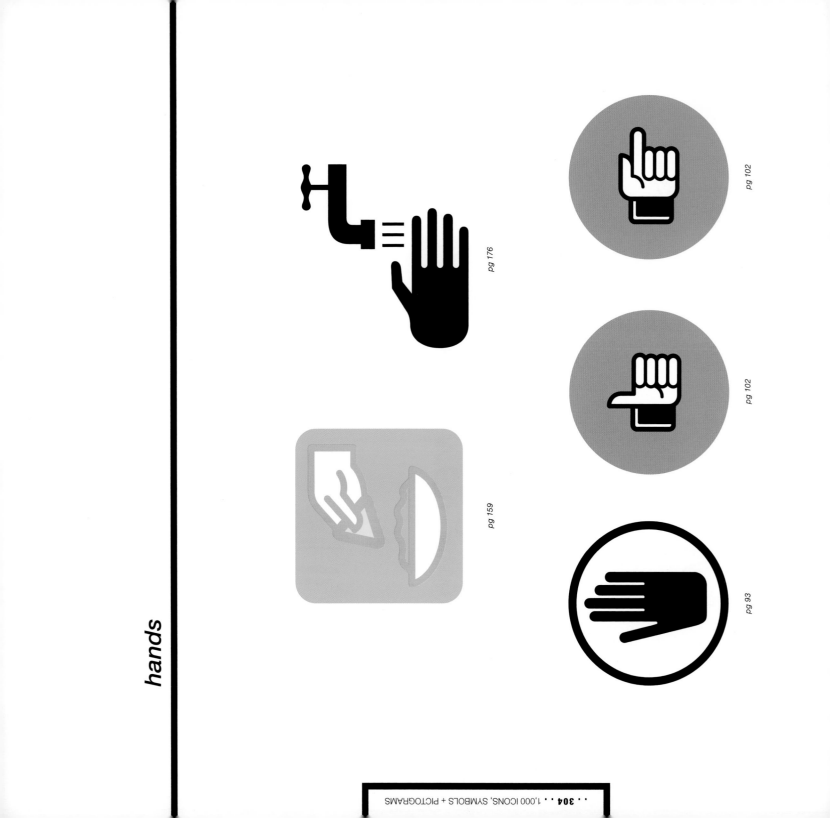

hands

pg 102

pg 102

pg 159

pg 176

pg 93

light bulbs

pg 126

pg 140

pg 215

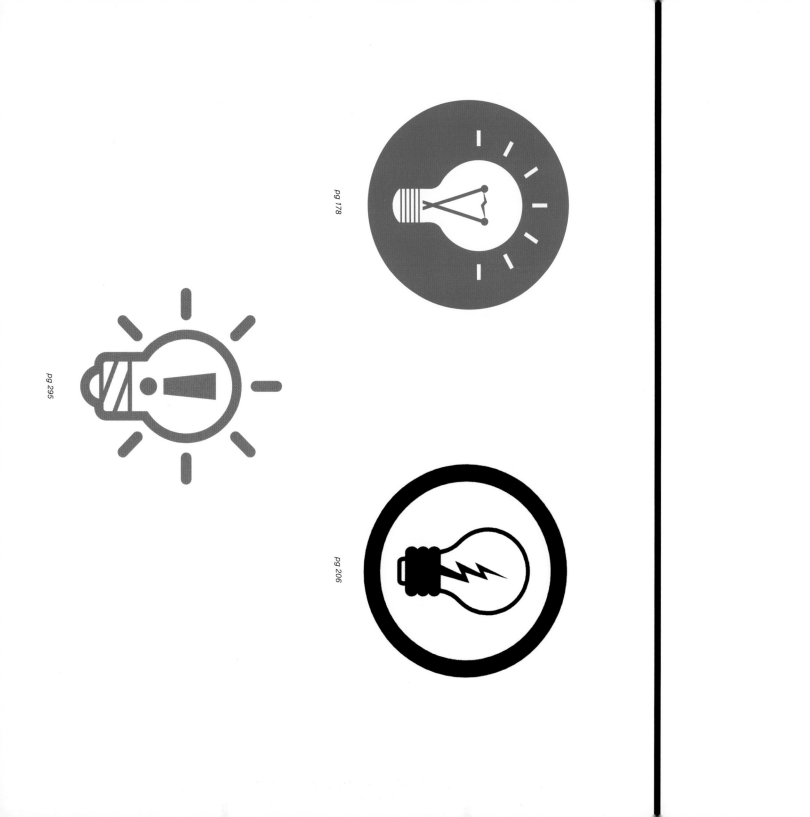

pg 178

pg 295

pg 206

animals

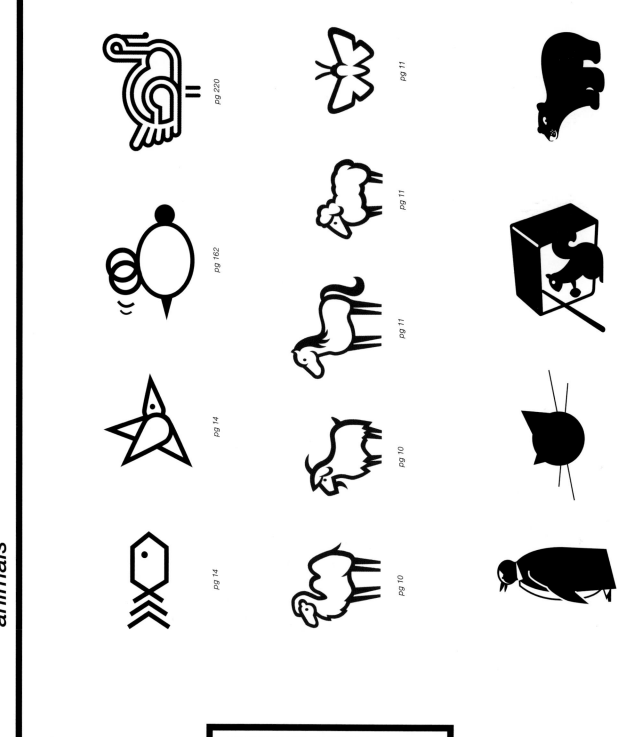

pg 220

pg 11

pg 96

pg 162

pg 11

pg 70

pg 14

pg 11

pg 168

pg 14

pg 10

pg 171

pg 10

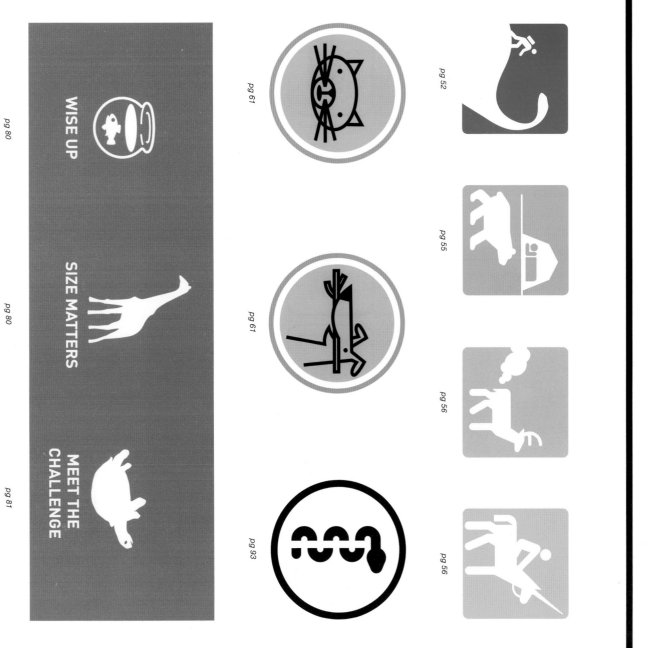

animals

pg 287

pg 139

pg 233

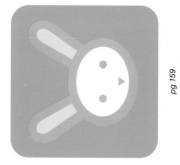

pg 159

pg 135

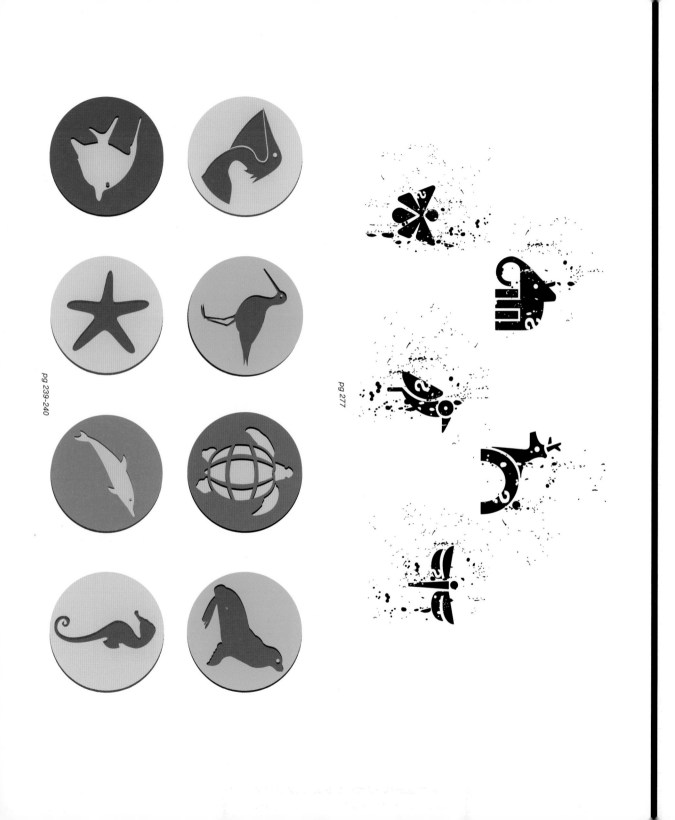

A

Atlas Communications
Travis Tom
958 Millbrook Ave., Suite 8
Aiken, SC 29803
USA
803.641.6899
ttom@atlascreates.com

0941–0960
Art Director: Atomic Kitchen Design
Designer: Travis Tom
Client: Atomic Kitchen Design

B

Blackcoffee
840 Summer St.
Boston, MA 02127
USA
617.268.1116
info@blackcoffee.com

0331–0337
Art Directors: Laura Savard and Mark Gallagher
Client: Naked Lion Brewing Company

0572
Art Directors: Laura Savard and Mark Gallagher
Client: SBR

0573–0574
Art Directors: Laura Savard and Mark Gallagher
Client: Blackcoffee

0702–0704
Art Director: Laura Savard and Mark Gallagher
Client: The Rockport Company

0705, 0992–1000
Art Directors: Laura Savard and Mark Gallagher
Client: Gary Tardiff Studio

0706–0707
Art Directors: Laura Savard and Mark Gallagher
Client: Blackcoffee

0839–0843
Art Directors: Laura Savard and Mark Gallagher
Client: Numark

0919–0921
Art Directors: Laura Savard and Mark Gallagher
Client: Conway Autoworks

Belyea
Patricia Belyea
1809 Seventh Ave., Suite 12150
Seattle, WA 98101
USA
206.682.4895
patricia@belyea.com

0584–0639
Art Director: Patricia Belyea
Designer: Caro Koegler
Client: Belyea

C

Cannondale Bicycle Corp.
John Lucas
16 Trowbridge Dr.
Bethel, CT 06801
USA
203.749.7094
john.lucas@cannondale.com

0051–0075
Art Director: Javier Alberich
Designer: Javier Alberich
Client: Cannondale Bicycle Corp. Creative Department

0088–0090
Art Director: Javier Alberich
Designer: Javier Alberich
Client: Cannondale Bicycle Corp. Creative Department

Chen Design Associates
Joshua C. Chen
589 Howard St., 4th Floor
San Francisco, CA 94105
USA
415.896.5338
info@chendesign.com

0036–0044
Art Director: Joshua C. Chen
Designer: Darlene Gibson
Client: Public Policy Institute of CA

0961–0966
Art Director: Joshua C. Chen
Client: CDA Press

Chris Rooney Illustration/Design
Chris Rooney
1317 Santa Fe Ave.
Berkeley, CA 94702
USA
415.827.3729
www.looneyrooney.com
looneyrooney@mindspring.com

0180–0194
Designer: Chris Rooney
Client: Chris Rooney

0506–0517
Designer: Chris Rooney
Client: Pacific Sun

0518–0523, 0575–0583
Designer: Chris Rooney
Client: Young & Rubicam

Dean Arts
Dean Hunsaker
2502 Dwight Way
Berkeley, CA 94704
USA
510.843.0586
dean@deanart.com

0195–0200
Art Director: Dean Hunsaker
Designer: Dean Hunsaker
Client: Regional Training Inst.

Dotzero Design
Jon Wippich
208 SW Stark St., #307
Portland, OR 97204
USA
503.892.9262
jonw@dotzerodesign.com

0085–0087
Designers: Jon Wippich and Karen Wippich
Client: Rejuvenation

0201–0212
Designers: Jon Wippich and Karen Wippich
Client: Bridgetown Printing

Dresser Johnson
Kevin Dresser
705 Manhattan Ave., #2
Brooklyn, NY 11222
USA
718.389.4830
dresser@dresserjohnson.com

0213–0214
Art Director: Andy Omel
Designer: Kevin Dresser
Client: Guitar World Acoustic Magazine

0215–0234
Art Director: Ed Pusz
Designer: Kevin Dresser
Client: The Museum of Modern Art

0656–0659
Designer: Kevin Dresser
Client: Two Twelve Associates

0660–0663
Art Director: Heidi Volpe
Designer: Kevin Dresser
Client: Outdoor Magazine

0696–0701
Art Director: Cindy Poulton
Designer: Kevin Dresser
Client: Working Mother Magazine

The Earth Institute @ Columbia University
Sunghee Kim
2910 Broadway, Hogan Hall B-16
New York, NY 10025
USA
212.854.0477
skim@ei.columbia.edu

0027–0035
Art Director: Mark A. Inglis
Designer: Sunghee Kim
Client: The Earth Institute @ Columbia University

F

Federico Panzano
C.soA. Gastaldi 19/34
Genoa, 16131
Italy
39.010.31.90.33
Federico.panzano@virgilio.it

0245–0298
Designer: Federico Panzano
Client: Hospital E.O. "Ospedali Galliera"

G

Gardner Design
Bill Gardner
3204 E. Douglas
Wichita, KS 67208
USA
316.691.8808
bill@gardnerdesign.com

0013–0026
Art Director: Brian Miller
Designer: Luke Bott
Client: Gardner Design

0489–0492
Art Director: Brian Miller
Designer: Luke Bott
Client: Gardner Design

0708–0713
Art Director: Brian Miller
Designer: Luke Bott
Client: Gardner Design

0801–0809
Art Director: Bill Gardner
Designer: Brian Miller
Client: Standard

0852–0871
Art Director: Brian Miller
Designer: Luke Bott
Client: Epic Apparel

0932–0937
Art Director: Brian Miller
Designer: Luke Bott
Client: Standard

GBH Design, Ltd
Piers Komlosy
Chiswick Station House
Burlington Ln.
London, W4 3HB, England
UK
44.0.20.8742.2277
studio@gregorybonnerhale.com

0235–0244
Art Directors: Peter Hale, Mark Bonner, and Jason Gregory
Designers: Peter Hale, Mark Bonner, Jason Gregory, Piers Komlosy, Pak Ying, and Russell Sanders
Client: PUMA

Gee + Chung Design
Earl Gee
38 Bryant St., Suite 100
San Francisco, CA 94105
USA
415.543.1192
earl@geechungdesign.com

0338–0344
Art Director: Earl Gee
Designer: Earl Gee
Client: Castile Ventures

0392–0461
Art Director: Earl Gee
Designer: Earl Gee
Client: Xinet, Inc.

Glitschka Studios
Von R. Glitschka
5165 Sycan Ct. SE
Salem, OR 97306
USA
971.223.6143
info@glitschka.com

0345–0384
Art Director: Von R. Glitschka
Designer: Von R. Glitschka
Client: self-published

0972–0986
Art Director: Von R. Glitschka
Designer: Von R. Glitschka
Client: www.creativelatitude.com

H

Winnie Hart/H
1055 St. Charles Ave., Suite 300
New Orleans, LA 70130
USA
504.522.6300
Winnie@thinkh.com

0793–0800
Art Director: Winnie Hart
Designers: Winnie Hart and Suzy Rivera
Client: Marsh Garden Décor

I

Ideas Frescas
Frida Larios
62 Caldecot Rd.
London, SE5 9RP, England
UK
44.793.035.4714
frida@ideas-frescas.com

0987–0991
Art Director: Frida Larios
Designer: Frida Larios
Client: MA Communication Design
Central Saint Martins College of Art and Design
The Embassy of El Salvador, in London

ideentity
Mirco Kurth
Uckendorfer Strasse 210
D-45886 Gelsenkirchen
Germany
49.209.39.42.38
info@ideentity.de

0938–0940
Art Director: Mirco Kurth
Designer: Mirco Kurth
Client: systemtrans e.k.

Inpraxis, Kommunikation + Design
Andreas Kranz
Nigerstrasse 4
81675 Munich
Germany
49.89.4443986
kontakt@inpraxis.com

0493–0499
Art Directors: Andréas Kranz, Christiane Schaffner
Client: Inpraxis, Kommunikation + Design

J

Joe Miller's Company
Joe Miller
3080 Olcott St., Suite 105a
Santa Clara, CA 95054
USA
408.988.2924
joecompany@aol.com

0895–0918
Designer: Joe Miller
Client: Hewlett-Packard

K

Kindred Design Studio
Steve Redmond
757 Shelburne Falls Rd.
Hinesburg, VT 05461
USA
802.482.5535
steve@kindredesign.com

0095–0119
Art Director: Steve Redmond
Designer: Steve Redmond
Client: IDX Corporation, Inc.

L

LSD
Gabriel Martínez
San Andres, 36 2 P6
Madrid 28004
Spain
34.915.943.813
Gabriel@lsdspace.com

0462–0488
Art Director: Gabriel Martínez
Designers: Gabriel Martínez and Paz Martin
Client: URJC Rey Juan Carlos University

0822–0827
Art Directors: Sonia Díaz and Gabriel Martínez
Designers: Sonia Díaz and Gabriel Martínez
Clients: Juan Carlos Ibáñes and Gema Díaz

M

mgmt. design
Alicia Cheng
55 Washington St., Suite 704
Brooklyn, NY 11201
USA
718.855.6262
Alicia@mgmtdesign.com

0174–0179
Art Director: Alicia Chen
Designers: Sarah Gephardt and Alicia Cheng
Client: *Metropolis* Magazine

0684–0695
Art Director: Alicia Chen
Client: *The New York Times*

Michael Graves Design Group
Patrick O'Leary
341 Nassau St.
Princeton, NJ 08540
USA
609.924.6409
poleary@michaelgraves.com

0091–0094
Art Director: Eric Bogner
Designer: Danielle Gingras
Client: Michael Graves Design Group

Mirko Ilić Corp.
Mirko Ilić
207 East 32nd St.
New York, NY 10016
USA
212.481.9737
studio@mirkoilic.com

0721–0756
Art Director: Mirko Ilić
Designer: Slavimir Stojanović
Client: Publikum

Mitch Anthony / Titanium
Mitch Anthony
126 Main St.
Northampton, MA 01020
USA
413.586.4304
mitch@element12.com

0885–0894
Art Director: Dann De Witt
Designer: Dann De Witt
Client: Numark

Muggie Ramadani Design Studio
Muggie Ramadani
Sortedam Dossering 55
Copenhagen, OE DK 2100
Denmark
45.26.70.89.89
contact@muggieramadani.com

0543–0562
Art Director: Muggie Ramadani
Designers: Muggie Ramadani and Frans Theis
Client: Blumoller A/S

P

Planet Propaganda
Travis Ott
605 Williamson St.
Madison, WI 53703
USA
608.256.0000
travis@planetpropaganda.com

0120–0173
Art Director: Kevin Wade
Designer: Jim Lasser
Client: Square Joint

PS Art & Design
Stephen A. Klema
69 Walnut St.
Winsted, CT 06098
USA
860.379.1579

0757–0762
Art Director: Stephen A. Klema
Client: Tunxis Community College

R

R&MAG Graphic Design
Raffaele Fontanella
Traversa del Pescatore 3
80053 Castellammare di Stabia
Italy
39.081.870.5053
info@remag.it

0299–0330
Art Directors: Raffaele Fontanella,
Maurizio Di Somma, and Marcello Cesar
Client: Ulysse Wellness Experience

Stoltze Design
Clifford Stoltze
49 Melcher St., 4th Fl.
Boston, MA 02210
USA
617.350.7109
clif@stoltze.com

0772–0775
Art Director: Clifford Stoltze
Designers: John Pietrafesa and Angelia Snellel
Client: Profit Logic

0872–0878
Art Director: Clifford Stoltze
Designer: Tammy Dotson
Client: Massachusetts College of Art

Studiovertex
Michael Lindsay
108 S Washington St., Suite 310
Seattle, WA 98104
USA
206.838.7240
michael@studio-vertex.com

0500–0505
Art Director: Michael Lindsay
Designer: Michael Lindsay
Client: PetroCard

Subcommunication
Sébastien Théraulaz
24 Av. Mont-Royal West, #1003
Montreal, PQ, H2T 2S2
Canada
514.845.9423
info@subcommunication.com

0563–0571
Art Director: Sébastien Théraulaz
Designer: Valérie Desrochers
Client: Chambly Martin Newspaper

0640–0641
Art Director: Sébastien Théraulaz
Designer: Valérie Desrochers
Client: Chambly Martin Newspaper

0642
Art Director: Sébastien Théraulaz
Designer: Valérie Desrochers
Client: Alexfilms

0643
Art Director: Sébastien Théraulaz
Designer: Sébastien Théraulaz
Client: Dominique Vitallis

Substance151
Ida Cheinman
2304 E. Baltimore St.
Baltimore, MD 21224
USA
410.732.8379
icheinman@substance151.com

0076–0084
Art Director: Ida Cheinman
Designer: Ida Cheinman
Client: The Kitchen

0524–0528
Art Directors: Ida Cheinman and Rick Salzman
Designers: Ida Cheinman and Rick Salzman
Client: LightWorks

T

The-Groop
Sharon Tani and Aldo Puicon
125 West 4th St., #103
Los Angeles, CA 90013
USA
213.613.0066
stani@thegroop.net
apuicon@thegroop.net

0388–0391
Creative Director: Jose Caballer
Designer: Aldo Puicon
Executive Producer: Sharon Tani
Client: The-Groop

TnTom Design
Travis Tom
2436 Apricot Ln.
Augusta, GA 30904
USA
706.495.8664
Tntom70@aol.com

0529–0542
Art Director: Amy Hawk
Designer: Travis Tom
Client: *HOW* Magazine

0676–0678
Art Director: Bob Klingler
Designer: Travis Tom
Client: Atomic-Fusion

BLACKCOFFEE® was founded in 1994 by Mark Gallagher and Laura Savard. The firm works with Acura, Cannondale, Converse, Hasbro, Kryptonite, MTV, Puma, Reebok, Salomon, Showtime, Timberland, and Zildjian, helping these companies transform brand position into brand aesthetic. They are authors of *The Best of Business Card Design 6* (Rockport, 2004) and are based in Boston, Massachusetts. For more information, please visit www.blackcoffee.com.